Development Macroeconomics in Latin America and Mexico

Development Macroeconomics in Latin America and Mexico

Essays on Monetary, Exchange Rate, and Fiscal Policies

Jaime Ros

palgrave
macmillan

DEVELOPMENT MACROECONOMICS IN LATIN AMERICA AND MEXICO

First published in 2015 by
PALGRAVE MACMILLAN®
in the United States—a division of St. Martin's Press LLC,
175 Fifth Avenue, New York, NY 10010.

Where this book is distributed in the UK, Europe and the rest of the world, this is by Palgrave Macmillan, a division of Macmillan Publishers Limited, registered in England, company number 785998, of Houndmills, Basingstoke, Hampshire RG21 6XS.

Palgrave Macmillan is the global academic imprint of the above companies and has companies and representatives throughout the world.

ISBN: 978–1–137–46526–9

Library of Congress Cataloging-in-Publication Data

Ros, Jaime.
[Essays. Selections]
Development macroeconomics in Latin America and Mexico : essays on monetary, exchange rate, and fiscal policies / Jaime Ros.
pages cm
Includes bibliographical references and index.
ISBN 978–1–137–46526–9 (hardback : alk. paper)
1. Monetary policy—Mexico. 2. Monetary policy—Latin America. 3. Fiscal policy—Mexico. 4. Fiscal policy—Latin America. 5. Economic development—Mexico. 6. Economic development—Latin America. I. Title.

HG665.R77 2014
339.5098—dc23 2014041241

A catalogue record of the book is available from the British Library.

Design by Newgen Knowledge Works (P) Ltd., Chennai, India.

First edition: April 2015

10 9 8 7 6 5 4 3 2 1

To Alejandra and Mike,
Diego and Fernanda,
and Pablo and Adriana

Contents

Figures and Tables

Figures

TABLES

Preface

This book is about some key questions in the economic development performance of Latin America in recent decades. It is a collection of essays in development macroeconomics highlighting the role of neglected macroeconomic factors in explaining the Latin American performance. Some of the chapters are unpublished papers presented at various conferences and workshops while others are revised and updated versions of documents prepared for the Economic Commission for Latin America and the Caribbean at the United Nations. All of them share a strong policy orientation. They are all about how Latin American countries can overcome an overall mediocre growth and development performance.

The book has benefited from the excellent research assistance of Santiago Capraro, Claudia Cordova, Joaquín Cervantes, Elizabeth González, David Maldonado, and Luis Angel Monroy Gómez Franco. Aranxa Sánchez and Víctor Vidal provided valuable help in preparing the index. Several colleagues provided comments on one or more chapters. I am indebted for that to Robert Blecker, José Casar, Rolando Cordera, Amitava Dutt, Carlos Ibarra, Juan Carlos Moreno-Brid, José Antonio Ocampo, Carlo Panico, Martín Rapetti, and Lance Taylor. My thanks go also to Palgrave Macmillan for an excellent job in converting the manuscript into a finished book and their continuous support and patience throughout the process.

Introduction

This book has two core themes: the disappointing average growth performance of Latin American economies during the post–market reforms period (since around 1990) and the significant diversity across countries around this average performance. More precisely, the main questions addressed are: (1) What explains that the Latin American subcontinent, which has gone further than other developing regions in the process of economic liberalization, has had such a poor and disappointing growth performance over the past 30 years; (2) What explains the diversity in growth performance across countries ranging from respectable growth rates in Dominican Republic, Chile, or Peru to very low growth rates in countries such as Mexico and Brazil. Why, in other words, do some Latin American economies grow faster than others?

Conventional explanations emphasize the role of institutional factors, human capital, or microeconomic factors, such as rigid labor markets, lack of competition, or insufficient international economic integration, affecting technical or economic efficiency in resource allocation. But these explanations leave unaddressed the Latin American paradox, that is, that in terms of institutions, human capital endowment or economic liberalization Latin American countries have been converging rapidly over the past 30 years while at the same time growth rates, after the lost decade of the 1980s, have been diverging. It is necessary for a full and convincing explanation to give answers to the two questions indicated above, answers that must be mutually consistent. The main argument of the book is that the variety of macroeconomic policies (fiscal, monetary, and exchange rate policies) together with the legacy and path-dependent outcomes of the shocks of the 1980s can give a satisfactory answer to these questions.

The main contributions of the book to the literature in the field are, first, to bring the attention of academics, practitioners, and policymakers to the neglected macroeconomic factors—having to do with levels of public investment (particularly in infrastructure), exchange rate management, financial intermediation, and sectoral investment incentives—that can account for both the unsatisfactory average growth performance of Latin American economies and the diversity around this average. Second, to stimulate and enrich the debate on the macroeconomic reform agenda that could revive the high growth rates that the region achieved in the postwar period up to the Latin American debt crisis of the 1980s.

OVERVIEW

The starting point in chapter 1 is that over the past 30 years Latin America has experienced a major overhaul in economic policies and institutions as well as in political institutions. As a result of these changes Latin America abandoned the paradigm that prevailed in the postwar period that placed the developmental State at the center of the strategy, with industrialization as the major objective. At the same time, when we compare the rankings in the growth tables for the periods 1950–1980 and 1990–2008, a "reversal of fortune" is apparent: countries, such as Chile, Argentina, Uruguay, which were in the bottom half in the growth table in the period 1950–1980, call them the "losers from ISI", tend to be in the upper half of the growth table in 1990–2008. And vice versa, countries such as Brazil, Mexico, Ecuador, Guatemala, the "winners from ISI", tend to be in the bottom half of the table for the same period. The chapter addresses the question of why this reversal of fortune has occurred despite (or perhaps because) the large degree of institutional and policy convergence across the region.

Chapter 2 presents a cross-country study for nine Latin American economies of Kaldor's "endogenous productivity growth" view according to which the long-term productivity growth rate in the whole economy is largely determined by the rate of capital accumulation in the increasing returns to scale sectors of the economy. This chapter also contrasts Kaldor's views with alternative explanations of productivity growth. A main argument is that conventional explanations that blame the slow growth performance of Latin America on a poor productivity growth performance simply get the direction of causality wrong.

Chapter 3 provides a theoretical foundation to the "profitability" or "development" channel postulated in the empirical literature on the real exchange rate and growth. In the models presented, a higher real exchange rate is favorable in the short run to capital accumulation and employment growth partly because it reduces the product wage in the traded goods sector with a positive effect on the sector's profitability. With endogenous productivity change, the employment gains are not reversed and the long-run value of the real wage increases as a result of the higher employment rate (which favors the diffusion of new technologies reducing labor costs) and the higher capital–labor ratio, which, through embodied technical progress and technological externalities, raises the economy's productivity.

After looking at the successful growth performance of several South American countries since 2003, chapter 4 looks at the medium- and long-term dangers involved in the natural resource boom. Indeed, the chapter addresses the subject of the developmental effects of a natural resource boom—the adverse effects of the Dutch disease and also the conditions under which such a boom could have favorable developmental effects—the experience of South America over the last decade, and the economic policy management issues of how to neutralize the adverse developmental effects of the Dutch disease.

Chapter 5 examines the comparative economic performance of Canada and Mexico since 1994 when these countries became the North American Free Trade Agreement (NAFTA) partners of the United States. The analysis gives a special attention to the behavior of the two economies during the international crisis and recession of 2008–2009, which had particularly severe effects in both countries given that their main trading partner, the United States, was the epicenter of the crisis. There were nonetheless interesting differences that the chapter relates to contrasts in the domestic policy responses (monetary, fiscal, and exchange rate management) in the two countries.

Chile and Mexico represent two extreme cases of growth performance in Latin America, the first being considered one of the few Latin American success stories and the second having one of the slowest growing economies in the region. Chapter 6 addresses the question of why this is so by reviewing the processes of economic liberalization and international integration in the two countries, the implications of different macroeconomic policy frameworks, and the role of China in the 2000s as a purchaser of raw materials from Chile and a formidable competitor of Mexico in the United States manufacturing markets.

Chapter 7 looks at the economic crisis of 2008–2009 in Mexico and beyond. It examines the size of the external demand shock in comparative perspective, the channels of transmission of the crisis (trade and capital flows), and the domestic policy response. It also puts the crisis in historical perspective by comparing it to the three recessions of the last quarter of the twentieth century (1983, 1986, and 1995) as well as to the Great Depression of the 1930s and asks why the crisis was so severe in the historical and international contexts. Finally, it discusses the changes in macroeconomic policy and development strategy that are necessary to sustain a pace of economic growth faster than in recent decades.

1

Institutional and Policy Convergence with Growth Divergence in Latin America*

This chapter compares the cross-country growth performance of Latin American countries during the postwar period of state-led industrialization and the economic liberalization period of the last three decades. The chapter describes the major overhaul in economic policies and institutions that Latin America experienced after the debt crisis of the 1980s. At the same time, we look at the growth performance over those two periods. When we compare the rankings in the growth tables for the periods 1950–1980 and 1990–2008, a "reversal of fortune" is apparent: countries, such as Chile, Argentina, Uruguay, that were in the bottom half in the growth table in the period 1950–1980, call them the "losers from ISI", tend to be in the upper half of the growth table in 1990–2008. And vice versa, countries such as Brazil, Mexico, Ecuador, Guatemala, the "winners from ISI", tend to be in the bottom half of the table for the same period. The chapter addresses the question of why this reversal of fortune has occurred despite (or perhaps because) the large degree of institutional and policy convergence across the region.

Economic and Political Reforms since the Debt Crisis: Institutional and Policy Convergence

In the first decades of the postwar period, Latin America embraced a paradigm that placed the developmental state at the center of the strategy, with industrialization, which was regarded at the time as critical to increase living standards, as the major objective. Over the past 30 years Latin America has experienced a major overhaul in economic policies and institutions as well as in political institutions. As a result, a "great transformation" has taken place, if we may appropriate Karl Polanyi's expression for events of a different scale.

The major policy changes included far-reaching programs of economic reforms in different areas. These changes gave a larger role to the private sector in the allocation of resources and greater scope to market forces and international competition, all this with the goal of entering a phase of strong export-led economic expansion. It is worth recalling what has happened. During and after the adjustment process to the debt crisis of 1982, monetary and fiscal policies were radically transformed. In 1980, in a group of 20 Latin American countries,[1] none had an independent central bank. By 2012, a majority of countries (11) had an independent central bank. In addition, in the largest countries (Brazil, Mexico, Chile, Colombia, and Peru) the central bank operated under an inflation-targeting regime with a floating exchange rate and price stability as its sole mandate.[2] Fiscal policy went through a similar overhaul. In 1980 no country had a balanced budget rule. By 2012, eight countries had a balanced budget law, generally a strict commitment to balance the budget every year with the exception of Chile, which had a structural budget rule that allowed for fiscal deficits during recessions provided that these were compensated by budget surpluses in boom periods (see Table 1.1).

Regarding structural reforms in other areas, the early and prominent components of the reform agenda were trade liberalization and deeper integration into the world economy based on comparative advantages, as well as a broad opening to foreign direct investment (FDI). As shown in Table 1.2, tariffs were sharply reduced and the tariff structure radically simplified as nontariff barriers were largely eliminated. The median average tariff which in 1985 was 42% fell to 5% in 2010 and the highest average tariff went down from 88% to 11%. These changes were

Table 1.1 Central Bank Independence and Fiscal Rules (2012)

Country	Central Bank Independence	Fiscal Rule
Brazil	Yes, since 1988[1]	B. B. since 2000
Chile	Yes, since 1989	Structural budget since 2000
El Salvador	Yes, since 1991	N. R.
Colombia	Yes, since 1992	B. B. since 1997
Honduras	Yes, since 1993	N. R.
Mexico	Yes, since 1993	B. B. since 2006
Peru	Yes, since 1993	B. B. since 1999
Paraguay	Yes, since 1995	N. R.
Uruguay	Yes, since 1995	N. R.
Ecuador	Yes, since 2002	B. B. since 2003
Guatemala	Yes, since 2002	N. R.
Argentina	Yes from 1992 to 2012	B. B. since 2000
Bolivia	No	N. R.
Costa Rica	No	N. R.
Cuba	No	N. R.
Dominican Republic	No	N. R.
Haiti	No	N. R.
Nicaragua	No	N. R.
Venezuela	No	N. R.
Panama	No Central Bank	B. B. since 2002

[1] Not formally independent but operates autonomously since 1988.
N. R. = No fiscal rule.
B. B. = Balanced budget.
Sources: IMF (2009), Jácome and Vázquez (2005), and Central Bank websites.

so far-reaching that, as argued in Ocampo and Ros (2011), the objective of setting low tariffs was achieved to a much greater extent than in the classical period of primary export-led growth in the late nineteenth and early twentieth centuries.

A wave of free trade agreements (FTAs) or custom unions took place with North American Free Trade Agreement (NAFTA), which came into effect in 1994), in the North and MERCOSUR (1991) in the South being the most important initiatives. Moreover, under the leadership of Mexico and Chile, a wave of bilateral or multilateral FTAs was launched. All this contributed to a sharp increase in the weight of international trade in the economy. As shown in Table 1.2, the share of exports and imports in gross domestic product (GDP) increased for the median country from 54.3% to 64.4%. Some spectacular increases were recorded

Table 1.2 Openness to International Trade and Foreign Investment

Country		
Average tariff (%)[1]	1985	2010
Median average tariff	42	5
Highest average tariff	88[b] (Dominican Republic)	11 (Venezuela)
Lowest average tariff	20 (Bolivia)	2 (C. Rica[a] and Nicaragua)
Foreign trade as % of GDP[2]	1980	2008
Median value	54.3	64.4
Highest value	177.9 (Panama)	156.5 (Panama)
Lowest value	11.5 (Argentina)	24.2 (Brasil)
FDI as % of total investment	1980	2009
Median value	4	13
Highest value	30 (Panama[c])	37 (Chile)
Lowest value	0 (Cuba and Venezuela)	–4 (Venezuela)

[1] Weighted mean to all products (%).
[2] Openness at 2005 constant prices (%).
[a] 2009, b: 1988, c: 1981.

Sources: For tariffs: Lora (2001), World Development Indicators.
For Foreign trade: PWT.
For FDI: UNCTADSTAT.

by Argentina (from 11.5% to 45.1%), Mexico (from 28.4% to 58.8%), Costa Rica (from 56.9% to 100.8%), and Paraguay (from 47.4% to 105.9%) (see Table 1.A.1 in Appendix). In turn, the relaxation of FDI regulations led to a sharp increase in the share of FDI in gross capital formation. The median country increased this share from 4% to 13% (see Table 1.2) and for some countries this share rose to over 30% (see Table 1.A.2 in Appendix).

Trade and FDI liberalization were accompanied, in addition, by the elimination of exchange controls and domestic financial liberalization. The latter included the liberalization of interest rates, the elimination of most forms of directed credit, and the reduction and simplification of reserve requirements on bank deposits. Although it was also accepted that financial liberalization required regulation to avoid the accumulation of excessive risks in the financial system, the full acceptance of the need for regulation only came after a fair number of domestic financial crises (in particular the Tequila crisis of 1994–1995).

Another component in the agenda of structural reforms was the privatization of a large set of public enterprises together with the opening to private investment of public services and utilities sectors. The more general deregulation of private economic activities was also part of the agenda. The privatization process was more gradual than in the case of trade liberalization and a number of countries kept public sector banks and a number of other firms, notably in oil and infrastructure services (water and sewage more than electricity and telecommunications).

There was, finally, an agenda of at least partial liberalization of labor markets, but here political factors limited the scope of the reform proposals (Murillo et al., 2011). Even then, as many as 13 countries in our group of 20 undertook changes in labor market regulations with the aim of making the labor market more flexible (see Table 1.3).

Table 1.3 Labor Market Reforms

Country	
Haiti	Yes (1984)
Brazil	Yes (1985)
Colombia	Yes (1990)
Guatemala	Yes (1990)
Argentina	Yes (1991)
Peru	Yes (1991)
Dominican Republic	Yes (1992)
Paraguay	Yes (1993)
El Salvador	Yes (1994)
Chile	Yes (1995)
Panama	Yes (1995)
Nicaragua	Yes (1996)
Ecuador	Yes (1997)
Venezuela	Yes (1999)
Bolivia	No
Costa Rica	No
Cuba	No
Honduras	No
Mexico	Yes (2011)
Uruguay	No

Source: Vega (2005); Lora and Pagés (1996) and NATLEX, International Labor Organization. Implementation year in parentheses.

Changes in political regimes went hand in hand with economic liberalization. Following Przeworski (2004) criteria to classify a political regime as authoritarian or democratic, Table 1.A.3 in the Appendix shows that in 1980 there were only four countries (Colombia, Costa Rica, Ecuador, and Venezuela) with democratic political regimes so that 85.1% of the population of the 20 Latin American countries lived under authoritarian regimes. In 2009, only one country (Cuba) continued to be authoritarian, representing 2% of the total population.

Moreover, perceptions about the rule of law in Latin America, available for 1996 to 2010 from Worldwide Government Indicators (WGI), show a steady improvement since 1996. The percentile rank of Latin American countries improved from 1996 to 2009 (see Table 1.4), with only six exceptions (Argentina,

Table 1.4 Percentile Rank for Rule of Law Indicator

Country	1996	2009	Change
Chile	85	87	+2
Uruguay	65	70	+5
Costa Rica	68	65	-3
Panama	49	51	+2
Brazil	40	50	+10
Colombia	20	41	+21
Dominican Republic	41	48	+9
Mexico	30	35	+5
Cuba	18	35	+17
Argentina	55	30	-25
Peru	30	30	0
El Salvador	20	22	+2
Nicaragua	35	22	-13
Honduras	20	20	0
Paraguay	21	19	-2
Bolivia	47	13	-34
Guatemala	12	13	+1
Ecuador	36	10	-26
Haiti	5	5	0
Venezuela	20	2	-18

Source: Worldwide Government Indicators (WGI). The WGI are produced by: Daniel Kaufmann, Brookings Institution, Aart Kraay, World Bank Development Research Group, Massimo Mastruzzi, World Bank Institute.

Bolivia, Ecuador, Nicaragua, Paraguay, and Venezuela) plus a minor fall for highly ranked Costa Rica.

AN INITIAL COMPARISON WITH THE PERIOD OF STATE-LED INDUSTRIALIZATION

The economic growth performance of Latin America since the 1980s is clearly weaker than that of the previous development phase. This is true even if we leave aside the "lost decade" of the 1980s. For the period 1990–2008, leaving aside also the recent crisis, the average of Latin America's per capita GDP growth rate has been 1.8% per year, well below the growth rate of the period 1950–1980 (2.7%) and less than the average growth rate of the world economy. The growth performance of GDP per worker, a gross measure of productivity, is even worse: 0.7% per year for 1990–2008 vs. 2.7% in 1950–1980. This means that most of the increase in GDP per capita since 1990 has been the result of the demographic bonus resulting from the slowdown of population growth (from 2.7% to 1.5%) in the face of a still relatively fast growth of the labor force (2.6% per year, a rate similar to the 2.8% of 1950–1980) (see Ros, 2009).

Table 1.5 indicates that only a few countries have experienced a dynamic growth of productivity at rates above 2% per year since 1990. Only four out of 19 countries (Dominican Republic, Peru, Chile, and Uruguay) had a better growth performance than in the period 1950–1980 while at the same time having an equal or faster growth than the United States for 1990–2008. Most countries recorded growth rates below that of the United States and a poorer growth performance in 1990–2008 than in 1950–1980. This poor overall productivity performance is not due to the absence of new dynamic and highly productive activities; it is rather the reflection of the rising share of low-productivity informal activities, as the dynamic highly productive sectors were unable to absorb a larger share of the labor force (Ros, 2011).

Table 1.5 Growth Performance 1990–2008 (Relative to 1950–1980)

		Above	Below
Relative to United States	Above	Dominican Rep. (2.9) Peru (2.9) Chile (2.3) Uruguay (2.2)	*Panama* (2.8) *El Salvador* (2.7) *Nicaragua* (2.1)
Average 1990–2008 (1.8%)	Below		Argentina (1.7) *Honduras* (1.5) Costa Rica (1.1) Brazil (1.0) Colombia (1.0) Guatemala (0.8) Bolivia (0.6) Mexico (0.6) *Paraguay* (–0.1) Ecuador (–0.1) Venezuela (–0.2) *Haiti* (–1.1)

In parentheses, growth rates (1990–2008) of GDP per person employed. Countries in italics show GDP per capita growth rate since for these countries GDP per person employed is not available.

Source: World Bank, World Development Indicators (WDI); Maddison (2007, 2009).

It is worth noting that, when looking across countries, there is no apparent relationship between the degree and timing of market liberalization and growth performance. The countries in the northwest box with two of the best performances are Chile, an early reformer, and the Dominican Republic, a late reformer. These two countries have also two very different macroeconomic frameworks: while Chile has an independent central bank and a structural balanced budget rule, the Dominican Republic has none of this (see Table 1.1). Interestingly, all of the fast-growing economies under state-led industrialization, with thoroughly liberalized economies, have now underperformed in relation to the past and the United States, with the major exceptions of the Dominican Republic and Panama. It also worth noting that this economic performance was affected not only by the poor results of the market reforms but also by worldwide macroeconomic turbulence. The collapse of growth during the lost decade of the 1980s was followed by a recovery in 1990–1997, although at a slower pace than during the years of state-led industrialization, and then by the "lost half decade" of 1998–2003. As a result, the relative position of Latin America in the world economy went back in 2003 to the levels of 1900 (see Ocampo and Ros, 2011). The combination of a new surge in external financing, the emergence of China as a new major purchaser of raw materials, and the increase in commodity prices, which had been absent since the 1970s, generated a new boom in 2004–2007, at a pace that was then more similar to that of the 1970s. The global crisis in 2008–2009 suddenly interrupted the recovery after 2003, bringing about a deep recession in 2009, second only to that of Central and Eastern Europe among the emerging and developing countries.

Causes of Slow Growth: Bad Governments or Good Governments with Bad Policies?

The factors explaining why some Latin American countries benefited more than others from the policy and institutional changes are to a large extent idiosyncratic. I will return below to this question. There were nevertheless some common factors behind the generalized failure to accelerate growth in the region, compared to the historical performance in 1950–1980. One such factor was a wrong diagnosis of the debt crisis. The reform overhaul was rooted in many policymakers' view that the 1982 debt crisis was the unavoidable consequence of the years of trade protectionism and heavy state intervention that had marked—and in their view distorted—Latin America's development during the postwar period. Thus, this crisis, which started with the Mexican moratorium of August 1982, was taken to be a crisis of the whole postwar strategy of state-led industrialization. In fact, this was simply wrong. In countries with a large public external debt, such as Brazil and Mexico, the source of the problem was unsustainable macroeconomic policies, in particular fiscal policy, which led to a debt crisis (like today's

European debt crisis) when the creditor banks realized that Mexico, facing a decline in oil prices since the beginning of 1981 and higher interest rates as a result of the tight monetary policy in the United States (the Volcker shock), would not be able to repay the debt. The same perceptions were then extended to the rest of Latin America. It is ironic that the diagnosis was most clearly contradicted by the problems of the Southern cone (Chile, Argentina, and Uruguay), which had abandoned import substitution and embarked on a path of economic liberalization since the mid-1970s and suffered a crisis in the early 1980s, not as a result of large fiscal deficits, but rather of increasing problems in their banking sectors and a rapid expansion of private external debt very much like the one that preceded the Tequila crisis of 1994–1995.

There were also problems of implementation coupled with an excessively optimistic view of the potential of structural reforms to trigger a resumption of growth. Trade liberalization, for example, was seen as a sufficient condition for export-led growth and was not accompanied by a depreciation of the real exchange rate as had been recommended by the advocates of export led growth such as Balassa and Baghwati, as well as, in fact, Williamson's Decalogue (where a competitive exchange rate was part of the ten-point program). Similarly, financial liberalization as it was undertaken proved a disaster leading eventually to the Tequila crisis. This was because the lessons from the Southern cone financial crisis of the early 1980s (which were analyzed by Díaz-Alejandro and Frenkel in the early 1980s) were simply not learnt.

The most important point to make here is that the slowdown in growth took place in the midst of positive institutional changes, including, as already emphasized, changes in the direction of the so-called inclusive political and economic institutions (democracy, the rule of law, and economic liberalization, see Acemoglu and Robinson, 2012). The failure to accelerate growth cannot be blamed on bad governments. It has to be the result of bad policies undertaken by good governments.

THE ROLE OF INDUSTRIAL POLICY AND MACROECONOMIC REFORM

Trade liberalization was accompanied by the dismantling of state intervention in productive development that had characterized the previous period, not only in the manufacturing sector but also in agricultural development. This vision was succinctly summarized by a lemma that was repeated in several contexts: "the best industrial policy is *not* to have an industrial policy." Trade liberalization and the dismantling of productive development policies were based on a number of arguments: the negative effects of protection on static efficiency (by moving the economy away from specialization according to comparative advantage and closing it off from external competition) as well as the encouragement of rent-seeking behavior as firms devoted resources to gaining advantages rather than increasing their efficiency. Technology policy, on which little progress had been made in the previous development phase (except, perhaps, in some agricultural research institutions), was also set aside, despite the fact that this is an element of intervention around which there is greater consensus.

Heterogeneous Growth Outcomes and the Reversal of Fortune

As shown in Table 1.6 when we compare the rankings in the growth tables for the periods 1950–1980 and 1990–2008, a "reversal of fortune" is apparent: countries, such as Chile, Argentina, and Uruguay, that were in the bottom half in the growth table in the period 1950–1980, call them the "losers from ISI", tend to be in the upper half of the growth table in 1990–2008. And vice versa, countries such as Brazil, Mexico, Ecuador, Guatemala, the winners from ISI, tend to be in the bottom half of the table for the period 1990–2008. In fact there are only a few visible exceptions to this pattern: the Dominican Republic and Costa Rica, which are in the upper half in both periods, and Venezuela and Haiti, which are in the bottom half

Table 1.6 GDP and GDP Per Capita Growth, 1950–1980 and 1990–2008

1950–1980				1990–2008				
GDPpC Ranking		GDP	GDPpC	Previous	GDPpC Ranking		GDP	GDPpC
1	*Brazil*	6.6	3.8	16	1	Chile	4.8	3.6
2	Panama	6.2	3.5	5	2	Dominican Rep.	5.2	3.6
3	Costa Rica	6.5	3.2	3	3	Costa Rica	4.7	2.9
4	*Mexico*	6.2	3.2	9	4	Peru	4.5	2.8
5	Dominican Rep.	5.7	2.6	18	5	Cuba	3.0	2.6
6	*Ecuador*	5.5	2.6	11	6	Argentina	2.8	1.7
7	Guatemala	5.2	2.5	7	7	Guatemala	3.7	1.6
8	*Colombia*	5.1	2.2	2	8	Panama	3.4	1.6
9	Peru	4.9	2.1	12	9	El Salvador	3.4	1.6
10	*Paraguay*	4.7	2.1	13	10	Nicaragua	3.8	1.6
11	*Argentina*	3.7	2.1	4	11	Mexico	3.0	1.6
12	*El Salvador*	5.0	2.0	14	12	Bolivia	3.5	1.4
13	*Nicaragua*	5.0	1.8	1	13	Brazil	2.8	1.4
14	Bolivia	3.8	1.5	19	14	Uruguay	1.9	1.3
15	Honduras	4.4	1.5	8	15	Colombia	2.8	1.1
16	*Chile*	3.2	1.1	15	16	Honduras	3.6	1.0
17	Venezuela	4.7	1.1	17	17	Venezuela	1.9	0.3
18	*Cuba*	2.5	0.6	10	18	Paraguay	2.2	–0.4
19	Uruguay	1.4	0.4	6	19	Ecuador	1.0	–0.9
20	Haïti	1.9	0.1	20	20	Haïti	0.2	–1.7
	L. America*	5.3	2.6			L. America*	3.0	1.5
	USA	3.6	2.3			USA	3.0	1.9

*Also includes Puerto Rico, Trinidad y Tobago and Jamaica.

Source: ***Angus Maddison project's web page*** (2012), Historical Statistics of the World Economy: 1–2008 AD, http://www.ggdc.net/MADDISON/oriindex.htm. References: Currency Unit: 1990 Geary-Khamis dollars. A: GDPpC Ranking 1950–1980.

in both periods. Excluding these four countries, the Spearman rank correlation coefficient is –0.11.

What accounts for differences in growth performance in that period and in the recent period? I will argue in this section that part of the explanation for this reversal of fortune has to do with the consequences of the abandonment of industrial policy. For that, we need to look at how industrial policy worked during the previous state-led industrialization period.

A first factor accounting for differences in growth rates and the relative success of industrial policy in the period of state-led industrialization has to do with the size of the economy. It cannot be a coincidence that Brazil and Mexico, the two most populous countries, were those able to sustain the highest rates of industrialization during the second, more difficult phase of import substitution, in which industrialization expanded into heavy intermediates (steel and petrochemicals) and capital goods as well as capital intensive consumer durables.[3] The size of their domestic markets is probably a major factor. For it allowed industrial sectors with high fixed costs (associated to their capital intensity), and as a result strong economies of scale, to be established while it attracted the foreign investment required to set up these capital and technology intensive industries. In other countries, the opportunities for import substitution were concentrated in light consumer goods and intermediate goods with low capital and technology intensity and attempts to go into the "difficult phase" could result in highly inefficient industrial sectors. In the case of the Southern cone economies with a relatively high degree of industrialization in 1950, the opportunities for easy import substitution were nonexistent or disappeared very soon (given, precisely, their relatively advanced industrial sectors).

A second factor affecting the efficiency of industrialization policies has to do with the nature of the domestic economy. Diaz-Alejandro (1988) highlights this factor in his comparison of the economic histories of Argentina and Brazil. Brazil was a dualistic economy, a Lewis-type economy. In Arthur Lewis's model of economic development there is a surplus of labor that generates an elastic supply of labor to the modern sector of the economy. This was important for the process of reallocation of labor in Brazil. The expansion of the industrial sector meant that the process of industrialization caused labor to move from low-productivity sectors to high-productivity sectors (from the "subsistence" to the industrial sector). These productivity gains were behind the rapid increases in GDP per worker and per capita. Argentina, by contrast, was a mature economy in which most sectors were modern and there was not a large subsistence sector. Productivity levels were similar across economic activities. This meant that the economy could not benefit from the reallocation of labor from low- to high-productivity sectors. Rather, the expansion of the industrial sector caused labor to be taken away from the modern export sector. Because industrialization crowded out labor in the export sector, the antiexport bias was higher in Argentina.

A third factor refers to the role of export promotion policies and exchange rate policy and how successful was the transition to the "mixed model" of import substitution cum export promotion. It is worth noting that four of the fast-growing economies are among the six that started experimenting with export promotion policies sometime in the 1960s or early 1970s (Bulmer-Thomas, 2003) and the two with crawling pegs (Colombia and Brazil). That is, all of the slow-growing economies with only two exceptions were not early adopters of export-promotion policies. In the case of the countries with large domestic markets (Brazil, Mexico, and to a lesser extent Colombia) the success of export promotion policies was facilitated by the smaller antiexport bias generated by the protection of intermediate and capital goods (to the extent that required tariffs were smaller). All this suggests a role in growth outcomes for the type of industrialization policy adopted.

It is not a coincidence that Brazil and Mexico, the only two countries to share these three features (large size, labor surpluses, and export promotion policy) are precisely the two countries at the top of the growth table (see Table 1.6).[4] It is these countries that benefited most from the productivity gains associated with the reallocation of labor toward the industrial sector and modern services. And I think this is the explanation for why the dismantling of industrial policy has harmed these two countries the most. In the period 1990–2008, they are clearly in the bottom half of the growth table.

This is part but not all the explanation for the "reversal of fortune" that characterizes the recent period since 1990 in comparison to the period 1950–1980. It turns out, as shown in Table 1.7, that the most prosperous economies since 1990 are those that have specialized in natural resource intensive products taking advantage of their static comparative advantage given by their abundance of natural resources. Table 1.7 ranks countries

Table 1.7 Natural Resource Abundance and Growth 1990–2008

Country	Net Exports of Primary Goods 2009[1]	Growth Rate 1990–2008[2]
Chile	29	2.3
Bolivia	27	0.6
Ecuador	24	-0.1
Honduras	22	*1.5*
Nicaragua	20	*2.1*
Paraguay	20	*-0.1*
Peru	18	2.9
Venezuela, RB	17	-0.2
Uruguay	13	2.2
Argentina	12	1.7
Guatemala	11	0.8
Colombia	10	1.0
Costa Rica	8	1.1
Mexico	6	0.6
Brazil	6	1.0
El Salvador	5	*2.7*
Panama	4	*2.8*
Dominican Rep.	3	2.9

The information for Cuba and Haiti was not available. GDP per capita in italics.
[1] Net exports of primary goods as % of GDP (WDI).
[2] Growth rate of GDP per person employed (WDI).
Source: WDI, World Bank.

according to net primary exports as a percentage of GDP, a frequently used indicator of abundance in natural resources (see, e.g., Sachs and Warner, 2001). The association between abundance and natural resources and growth since 1990 is remarkable. These resource-rich economies were the ones able to compensate the employment and output losses in manufacturing industries, an option that was not available to countries that were poorer in natural resources. There were, of course, exceptions such as the Dominican Republic a country whose comparatives advantages are assembly of manufactures and tourism given by its location advantage.

The dismantlement of industrial policy was thus a big mistake. The best industrial policy, at least in the larger and poorer economies in natural resources, is not "not to have an industrial policy."

Appreciating Real Exchange Rates, Falling Industrial Profitability, and Deindustrialization

Another big mistake has been to let real exchange rates appreciate rather than compensating trade liberalization and the dismantling of industrial policy with a relatively undervalued real exchange. This has meant that the region has been recurrently infected by the Dutch disease (appreciation caused by booms of natural resource intensive exports) and by the "Mexican disease" (appreciation caused by massive capital inflows).

Let us look at the Dutch disease in recent periods. The fast-growing countries included in Table 1.8 are either those rich in natural resources (Chile, Peru, and Uruguay) or those which avoided a dramatic process of deindustrialization (Dominican Republic, Panama, and El Salvador).

In the case of the natural resource–rich countries, the dynamism of the Chinese economy and of the world demand for raw materials have had so far favorable short-term effects on economic growth (see chapter 4 in this book). The medium- and longer-term developmental consequences of the raw

Table 1.8 Share of Manufacturing in GDP (%)[1]

Country	1990	2010[2]	Change
Uruguay	28.0	15.0	-13.0
Brazil	27.4[a]	15.8	-11.6
Chile	19.6	11.5	-8.1
Argentina	26.8	20.5	-6.3
Colombia	20.6	15.1	-5.5
Costa Rica	22.6	17.4	-5.2
Bolivia	18.5	13.9	-4.6
Paraguay	16.8	12.2	-4.6
Panama	9.7	6.1	-3.6
Mexico	20.8	18.1	-2.7
El Salvador	22.1	20.6	-1.5
Peru	17.8	16.6	-1.2
Venezuela, RB	14.9	14.7	-0.2
Cuba	7.7	9.6	1.9
Honduras	16.3	18.4	2.1
Dominican Rep.	18.0	24.1	6.1
Median	19.0	15.8	-3.2
Mean	19.2	15.7	-3.5

[1] Manufacturing value added as percentage of gross value added at factor cost.
[a] Average of 1989 and 1991.
[2] 2010 or last available data.
Source: WDI, World Bank.

materials export boom will depend, however, on its effects on real exchange rates and the profitability of the nonresource-intensive tradable goods sectors, that is on whether a Dutch disease is developing in the region. As shown in chapter 4, the raw materials export boom has been accompanied by a substantial appreciation of real exchange rates in Latin America sometime after the beginning of the past decade, only briefly interrupted by the temporary depreciations that took place in 2008 and early 2009 as a consequence of the international financial crisis, the "flight to quality," and the increase in risk spreads in emerging markets.

Chapter 4 assesses the extent of appreciation by comparing the level of the real exchange rate in 2010 with its average level for the period 2002–2008 and the minimum level (i.e., the most appreciated level) in the 1990s. With the exception of Argentina, real exchange rates in 2010 were similar or lower than the minimum levels of the 1990s and well below (including Argentina) the average levels of 2002–2008. The primary exports boom has led to a decline in the profitability of the industrial sector. In several South American countries, unit labor costs in dollars tended to increase after 2002–2003 in a substantial and sustained way suggesting that, at least for the labor intensive tradable goods sectors, there is an important problem of competitiveness and profitability.

Can Macroeconomic Policy Be a Substitute for Industrial Policy?

The relationship between the real exchange rate and the rate of economic growth has been receiving a great deal of attention in recent times after the extraordinarily high growth rates achieved by countries that have deliberately undervalued their real exchange rates (this is the case of China) and the slow growth rates experienced by a large number of countries with overvalued exchange rates (see chapter 3). In the absence of an industrial policy, and given the current institutional weakness to implement such a policy, can macroeconomic policy be a good substitute?

As noted by Kaldor and others, a high real exchange rate is equivalent to a tariff on imports and an export subsidy. Both of these, tariff and subsidy, benefit the tradable goods sectors, manufacturing being the largest of them in most countries. To counteract the adverse developmental effects of the Dutch and Mexican diseases and in this way act as a partial substitute for industrial policy, macroeconomic policy must fulfill certain requirements.

Since the adverse effects of those diseases arise mostly from the real exchange appreciation that accompanies the expansion of primary exports or the massive capital inflows and its crowding out effects on nonresource-based tradable sectors, exchange rate policy has a crucial role to play in neutralizing these effects.

If this is so, the inflation targeting regimes currently fashionable in Latin America are not well prepared for the task of addressing those adverse developmental consequences. In fact, under this regime there seems to be a built in bias toward the appreciation of the exchange rate. As discussed in chapter 4, the evolution of real exchange rates in Latin America in three groups of countries according to monetary policy regime (inflation targeting cum floating exchange rates, dollarized regimes, and others) suggests that the trend toward real appreciation in the period 2002–2008 was much more marked in countries with inflation targeting regimes was in the other two groups of countries.

As argued more fully in chapter 4, the task of counteracting the Dutch and Mexican diseases requires not only giving monetary policy a greater room for maneuver in order to target the exchange rate but also policy coordination through the help, in particular, of fiscal policy and wage management policies. Indeed, fiscal policy may have to play a more preponderant role in managing domestic aggregate demand and in restraining, in particular, inflationary pressures in the non-tradable goods sectors (see, on the subject, Eichengreen, 2007; Frenkel, 2008; Rapetti, 2011). Since part of the real appreciation associated to the Dutch disease arises from the spending out of natural resource rents on nontradable goods and services, or, in the case of the Mexican disease, from the expansion of credit resulting from massive capital inflows, counteracting this may require an increase in the fiscal surplus in order to moderate the pace of nontradable demand growth. The required increase in the fiscal surplus can be generated through tariffs or taxes on the primary exports, which are at the origin of the Dutch disease (see, on the subject, Bresser-Pereira, 2008, 2011).

Wage management policies that coordinate the pace of real wage increases with the rate of productivity growth in the tradable goods sector can also help in restraining inflationary pressures in nontradable goods prices and in containing the growth of unit labor costs, thus preventing the fall in profitability and capital accumulation in nonresource-intensive tradable goods sectors. As argued in chapter 3, while a higher real exchange rate implies that in the short run real wages are lower than otherwise, it will nevertheless lead to higher real consumption wages in long-run equilibrium as a result of the endogenous productivity growth effects of capital accumulation in the tradable goods sectors and of the absorption of employment from nontradable goods sectors. The mechanisms connecting an initially higher real exchange rate and a higher value of the real wage in the steady state are the presence of increasing returns to scale in the tradable goods sector and of diminishing returns to labor in the nontradable goods activities.

APPENDIX

Table 1.A.1 Foreign Trade as % of GDP

Country	1980	2008
Argentina	11.5	45.1
Bolivia	46.0	82.9
Brazil	15.9	24.2
Chile	49.3	85.7
Colombia	31.2	40.0
Costa Rica	56.9	100.8
Cuba	62.8	44.9
Dominican Rep.	78.8	64.7
Ecuador	50.8	75.5
El Salvador	67.4	73.6
Guatemala	66.5	64.1
Haiti	78.8	54.8
Honduras	100.0	136.5
México	28.4	58.8
Nicaragua	61.2	104.7
Panama	177.9	156.5
Paraguay	47.4	105.9
Peru	56.4	53.4
Uruguay	36.7	62.7
Venezuela	52.2	51.8
Average	**58.8**	**74.3**

Source: PWT. Openness at 2005 constant prices (%).

Table 1.A.2 FDI as % of Gross Fixed Capital Formation

Country	1980	2009
Argentina	4	6
Bolivia	12	15
Brazil	4	10
Chile	4	37
Colombia	2	13
Costa Rica	4	22
Cuba	0	0
Dominican Republic	6	32
Ecuador	3	3
El Salvador	4	13
Guatemala	8	12
Haiti	5	5
Honduras	1	15
Mexico	4	8
Nicaragua	6	22
Panama[a]	30	30
Paraguay	3	8
Peru	1	19
Uruguay	12	25
Venezuela	0	−4

[a] 1981.

Source: UNCTADSTAT.

Table 1.A.3 Type of Political Regime and Population by Country 1980 and 2009

Country	Authoritarian Regime 1980	Population by 1980 (Thousands)	Authoritarian Regime 2009	Population by 2009 (thousands)
Mexico	Yes	68,347	No	111,212
Chile	Yes	11,094	No	16,602
Argentina	Yes	28,370	No	40,914
Cuba	Yes	9,653	Yes	11,110
Costa Rica	No	2,299	No	4,455
Uruguay	Yes	2,930	No	3,294
Panama	Yes	1,960	No	3,360
Venezuela	No	14,768	No	27,191
Colombia	No	26,631	No	43,677
Brazil	Yes	123,020	No	198,739
El Salvador	Yes	4,566	No	6,031
Peru	Yes	17,295	No	28,647
Guatemala	Yes	6,650	No	13,277
Ecuador	No	7,920	No	14,573
Honduras	Yes	3,402	No	7,834
Paraguay	Yes	3,196	No	6,291
Bolivia	Yes	5,441	No	9,775
Nicaragua	Yes	2,806	No	5,541
Haiti	Yes	5,200	No	9,778
	Latin American population living under an authoritarian regime in 1980		Latin American population living under an authoritarian regime in 2009	
	85.1%		2.0%	

The sum of the population of the 19 countries was considered as the total population of Latin.

Note: To determine if the political regime was a democratic or an authoritarian one the criteria of Przeworski (2004) was followed.

Source: Prepared by the author with information from Heston, Alan; Robert Summers and Bettina Aten, Penn World Table Version 7.0, Center for International Comparisons of Production, Income and Prices at the University of Pennsylvania, May 2011.

2

Productivity and Growth: Stylized Facts and Kaldor's Laws in Latin America*

Output and productivity growth in Latin America, as we have seen in chapter I, have been slow and disappointing during the last three decades, especially when considering the great expectations created by the change in its development policies. At the same time, there is a great variety of performances within the region. Most economies have grown less than the world average, and a majority among them less than in the 1950–1980 period, but about seven (out of 18) countries have recorded a per capita GDP growth rate greater than the world average and in six of them greater than in the three decades that preceded the debt crisis of the 1980s. This chapter examines the causes of the economic growth differences in Latin America with special emphasis on the differential productivity performance.

The approach adopted to examine these different performances goes back to Allyn Young (1928) and Kaldor (1967) visions of the development process, a vision that has been rehabilitated by modern endogenous growth theory.[1] It sees productivity growth as endogenous, a by-product to a large extent of the growth of output and physical capital accumulation themselves. This approach is based on the one hand on Kaldor's technical progress function (Kaldor, 1957) and, on the other, in so called Verdoorn's law, rehabilitated by Kaldor in later writings (Kaldor, 1966, 1967, 1968), which explains productivity growth by the rate of output growth within manufacturing industry as a result of the presence of increasing returns to scale in manufacturing.[2]

A Verdoorn law, or as is often called Kaldor's third law, can also be established for the economy as a whole. In addition to the mechanisms prevailing in manufacturing, the absorption of labor force in the high productivity sectors of the economy is another way in which the expansion of production indirectly influences the average rate of productivity growth in the economy as a whole. This occurs as a result of productivity gains generated by the reallocation of labor and the fact that in the low productivity sectors, characterized by the absence of increasing returns to scale and the presence of surplus labor, the higher is the rate of growth of employment the lower tends to be productivity growth. Thus capital accumulation and the rate of expansion of the modern, high-productivity sectors have also an influence on productivity change in the low-productivity sectors and indirectly affect the growth rate of global productivity.

This chapter discusses the main stylized facts of Latin America's economic development since 1950 in the first section. Then it presents the Kaldorian vision of the growth process in the second section and examines empirically the main intersectoral relationships between output, productivity, and employment in the third section. Fourth section concludes by examining the interactions between growth, capital accumulation and productivity.

Some Stylized Facts of Latin America's Economic Development since 1950

Growth Accounting

As already mentioned in chapter 1, Latin America's output growth has been slow over the last decades. Growth of output per worker has even been lower: 0.7% per year from 1990 to 2008 compared to 2.7% in 1950–1980, so that the small increase in GDP per capita since 1990 has been largely the result of the demographic bonus originating in the population growth slowdown from 2.7% to 1.5% per year in the context of a still rapid labor force growth (2.6% per year, similar to 2.8% of the period 1950–1980) (Ros, 2009). Total factor productivity growth (TFP, simple average for 11 countries with available information), which had grown at a rate of 1.6% per year between 1950 and 1980, slowed down to a rate of 0.1% between 1980 and 2008 (and to 0.8% between 1990 and 2008).[3] Just as in the case of output growth, the changes in labor productivity and TFP show a similar degree of divergence within the region. It is worth noting, however, that if we measure labor productivity growth between peak years in order to reflect long-run trends, labor productivity growth slows down in the 11 countries with available information when comparing the period since the early 1990s to the period from the early 1950s to the debt crisis of the 1980s (see Table 2.1). This is unlike what happens to GDP per capita growth, which, as already mentioned, accelerates in some countries between those two periods. The magnitude of the slowdown in labor productivity growth varies from country to country going from less than 1 percentage point in Argentina, Chile, Colombia, and Bolivia to more than 2 percentage points in Brazil, Mexico, and Ecuador. Something similar occurs with TFP growth that slows down (or stagnates) in all countries except Argentina and Venezuela since the early 1990s (Table 2.1).

A common assertion is that the slowdown in labor productivity growth in Latin America is largely "explained" by the slowdown in TFP growth rather than the slowdown in the accumulation of capital per worker, a view that appears prominently in the IDB study on growth and productivity in Latin America (Pagés, 2010). It has been said, for example, that in the case of Mexico most of the fall in the GDP growth rate after the debt crisis is associated with the reduction in TFP growth (see Faal, 2005, among others). As shown in Table 2.1, this is indeed the case of Mexico: while labor productivity growth fell by 2.4 percentage points between 1951–1981 and 1994–2011,

Table 2.1 Comparative Performance of the Growth of Labor Productivity, Capital Per Worker, and TFP

	Output Per Worker		Capital Per Worker		TFP	
	1952–1980	1987–2008	1952–1980	1987–2008	1952–1980	1987–2008
Brazil	4.58	0.85	3.11	1.07	3.19	0.36
	1951–1981	1994–2011	1951–1981	1994–2011	1951–1981	1994–2011
Mexico	3.15	0.79	1.92	1.68	2.06	-0.24
	1954–1981	1988–2008	1954–1981	1988–2008	1954–1981	1988–2008
Ecuador	3.02	0.49	1.44	-0.03	2.05	0.51
	1953–1981	1992–2007	1953–1981	1992–2007	1953–1981	1992–2007
Chile	2.47	1.91	4.35	3.55	0.02	-0.06
	1954–1981	1987–2008	1954–1981	1987–2008	1954–1981	1987–2008
Peru	2.45	0.89	2.15	1.38	1.52	0.04
	1955–1979	1986–2011	1955–1979	1986–2011	1955–1979	1986–2011
Costa Rica	2.39	1.12	2.47	0.66	1.48	0.87
	1950–1980	1991–2011	1950–1980	1991–2011	1950–1980	1991–2011
Guatemala	2.15	0.20	0.58	-0.01	1.84	0.21
	1951–1980	1987–2008	1951–1980	1987–2008	1951–1980	1987–2008
Argentina	2.01	1.95	2.97	0.64	0.56	1.60
	1954–1980	1989–2007	1954–1980	1989–2007	1954–1980	1989–2007
Colombia	1.99	0.51	1.30	1.20	1.36	-0.09
	1952–1981	1992–2008	1952–1981	1992–2008	1952–1981	1992–2008
Venezuela	1.88	0.31	3.16	-0.30	0.02	0.49
	1952–1975	1989–2009	1952–1975	1989–2009	1952–1975	1989–2009
Bolivia	1.59	1.22	1.13	0.35	1.05	1.05

Source: PWT 8.0. Logarithmic growth rates estimated between peak years. See Appendix.

TFP growth fell by 2.3 percentage points. Similar cases, albeit with a less pronounced fall in TFP growth, are Guatemala and Peru. However, reality is more complex for other countries. In some, such as Colombia, Brazil, and Ecuador, the slowdown in labor productivity growth is "explained" by reductions in both capital accumulation per worker and TFP growth. In other countries the role of capital accumulation dominates: in Chile and Bolivia the slowdown in labor productivity growth is associated to the fall in capital accumulation per worker while in Venezuela and Argentina TFP growth in fact accelerates slightly in the midst of a sharp fall in the growth of both capital per worker and output per worker.

The episodes of fastest growth in our sample of countries, all of them (except Peru, 2003–2008, and Chile, 1992–1998) during the three decades prior to the debt crisis, are associated to fast TFP growth. As shown in Table 2.2, considering periods that comprise full economic cycles (see Appendix), the ten episodes with output growth higher than 6% per year include the periods with fastest TFP growth, five of them at rates higher than 2% per year. And vice versa, the 13 episodes with output growth lower than 2% per year (the great majority during the lost decade of the 1980s) all show, with only two exceptions, negative TFP growth rates (see Table 2.3).

Table 2.2 Episodes of Fastest Growth (Annual growth rates)

	GDP	TFP	Industry	Manufacturing
Brazil, 1961–1974	7.8	3.3	8.1	7.9
Venezuela, 1952–1957	7.5	0.9	10.6	13.2
Brazil, 1952–1961	7.4	3.9	9.1	9.7
Peru, 2003–2008	7.4	2.7	8.6	8.0
Brazil, 1974–1980	6.6	1.9	7.8	6.5
Mexico, 1970–1981	6.6	0.8	7.1	6.7
Chile, 1992–1998	6.5	1.5	5.1	4.0
Mexico, 1957–1964	6.2	3.1	7.4	7.7
Mexico, 1951–1957	6.1	3.9	6.6	6.1
Costa Rica, 1970–1979	6.0	0.3	8.4	7.9

Source: PWT 8.0 and Timmer and de Vries (2007).

Table 2.3 Episodes of Slowest Growth (Annual Growth Rates)

	GDP	TFP	Industry	Manufacturing
Bolivia, 1952–1957	-1.9	-0.5	-5.0	-5.2
Argentina, 1980–1987	-0.1	-1.7	-1.0	-0.6
Bolivia, 1975–1989	0.5	-1.7	0.4	0.6
Peru, 1987–1997	1.0	-1.2	1.5	-0.2
Costa Rica, 1979–1986	1.1	-0.9	0.6	1.3
Venezuela, 1992–1998	1.3	-1.2	-0.1	0.4
Venezuela, 1976–1981	1.5	-3.2	1.7	2.2
Brazil, 1987–1995	1.7	0.0	0.2	0.3
Argentina, 1974–1980	1.8	-0.4	1.3	-0.6
Mexico, 1981–1994	1.8	-1.2	1.7	1.9
Peru, 1981–1987	1.8	-1.6	2.3	2.6
Brazil, 1995–2001	1.9	-0.2	1.3	0.9
Bolivia, 1967–1975	1.9	0.2	5.8	5.6

Source: PWT 8.0 and Timmer and de Vries (2007).

The close relationship between output and TFP growth is confirmed by regressing the growth of output per worker ($\widehat{LP}$) against the rate of growth of capital per worker ($\widehat{K/L}$) and TFP growth ($\widehat{TFP}$) for the 78 country growth episodes in our sample. The coefficient of the variable $\widehat{TFP}$ is positive and highly significant confirming clearly that there are important differences in the growth of TFP across episodes that are related to differences in the growth of output per worker. The regression results are as follows:

$$\widehat{LP} = -0.003 + 0.53(\widehat{K/L}) + 0.98\widehat{TFP} \quad \hat{R}^2_{(adj)}. = 0.99 N = 78$$
$$(-0.12)\ (53.4) \qquad (71.4)$$

t-statistics in parentheses.

This close correlation between output and TFP growth does not establish in which direction causality runs. Indeed, the variation over time in TFP growth is hard to explain as a phenomenon independent from the growth of output. It is hard to explain for example why did TFP fall in the 1980s in all countries except Colombia and Chile (see Table 2.4) independently of the behavior of output and it would be absurd to conclude

Table 2.4 TFP during the Lost Decade (Annual Rates of Growth)

	Output	TFP
Argentina, 1980–1987	-0.1	-1.7
Bolivia, 1975–1989	0.5	-1.7
Peru, 1981–1987	1.8	-1.6
Ecuador, 1981–1988	1.9	-1.3
Brazil, 1980–1987	2.4	-1.3
Mexico, 1981–1994	1.8	-1.2
Guatemala, 1980–1991	1.1	-1.0
Costa Rica, 1979–1986	1.1	-0.9
Venezuela, 1981–1992	2.0	-0.3
Chile, 1981–1992	3.8	0.5
Colombia, 1980–1989	3.3	1.0

Source: PWT 8.0 and Timmer and de Vries (2007).

that the fall was the result of technological regress when many other developing countries (in East Asia in particular) did not suffer such a reduction in TFP.[4] It is far more reasonable to attribute the fall in TFP in the nine countries in which it did to the reduction in output itself in conditions of acute macroeconomic instability.

Growth and Industrialization

Let's go back to the rapid and slow growth episodes. As can be seen in Table 2.2, the episodes of rapid growth are nearly all periods in which industrial production grew at a faster rate than total GDP, that is to say the economy industrialized. These are also the periods in which TFP and labor productivity in the economy as a whole grew rapidly. Only in one case (Chile, 1992–1998) the growth of the industrial output was lower than total GDP growth. Note that Peru in recent years is no exception: its recent rapid growth is associated with a high level of industrial and manufacturing dynamism. In contrast, the episodes of slow growth of total output and TFP are periods of slow industrial output growth and, in general, de-industrialization with an industrial product that grows less than GDP, as shown in Table 2.3.

Human Capital and Growth

A paradoxical result is that the accumulation of human capital is not positively related with the growth of TFP. In a regression of TFP growth with respect to the rate of growth of human capital, the two indicators of the latter variable present, paradoxically, negative and statistically significant coefficients (Table 2.5). A higher rate of accumulation of human capital is associated to a decrease in the growth of the TFP and vice versa.

A way to corroborate the sign and significance of the accumulation of human capital ($\widehat{H}$) is to run growth accounting regressions of the type of Benhabib and Spiegel (1994, with and without country fixed effects) and see if $\widehat{H}$ is significant. Table 2.6 presents the results of running real GDP growth ($\widehat{Y}$) against the rates of growth of physical capital ($\widehat{K}$), employment ($\widehat{L}$) and human capital ($\widehat{H}$): $\widehat{Y} = a + b\widehat{K} + c\widehat{L} + d\widehat{H}$

Unlike physical capital accumulation and employment growth, both with positive and highly significant coefficients, the growth of human capital coefficient remains negative and significant. As with the results of Benhabib and Spiegel for a broader sample of countries, this throws doubts on the explanatory power of exercises of growth accounting in which H enters as a factor in the production function. It is worth noting that in

Table 2.5 The Accumulation of Human Capital as a Determinant of TFP Growth

	Without Fixed Effects	With Fixed Effect by Country	Without Fixed Effects	With Fixed Effect by Country
Constant	1.66	1.83	1.36	1.56
	(5.06)	(5.34)	(4.67)	(5.09)
$\widehat{H}_1$	−1.02	−1.20		
	(−3.44)	(−3.82)		
$\widehat{H}_2$			−0.36	−0.47
			(−2.84)	(−3.41)
$R^2_{(aj)}$	0.12	0.12	0.08	0.08

Number of observations = 78. t statistics between parentheses.

$\widehat{H}_1$: Rate of growth of human capital adjusted by returns to education (PWT 8.0).

$\widehat{H}_2$: Rate of growth of human capital measured by years of schooling (Barro-Lee, with interpolated data).

Table 2.6 Growth Accounting

	Without Fixed Effects	With Fixed Effect by Country	Without Fixed Effects	With Fixed Effect by Country
Constant	1.30	1.26	1.02	0.97
	(2.80)	(2.47)	(2.26)	(1.95)
$\widehat{K}$	0.61	0.69	0.61	0.71
	(6.70)	(6.41)	(6.57)	(6.46)
$\widehat{L}$	0.48	0.44	0.47	0.44
	(4.39)	(3.77)	(4.25)	(3.62)
$\widehat{H}_1$	-1.03	-1.23		
	(-3.36)	(-3.75)		
$\widehat{H}_2$			-0.37	-0.50
			(-2.82)	(-3.48)
$R^2_{(aj)}$	0.51	0.50	0.49	0.49

Number of comments = 78. T Statistics between parentheses.
$\widehat{H}_1$: rate of growth of human capital adjusted by returns to education (PWT 8.0)
$\widehat{H}_2$: rate of growth of human capital measured by years of schooling (Barro-Lee, with interpolated data).

our regressions the coefficients of capital and labor add to more than unity, possibly an indication of the presence of increasing returns to scale.

The explanation of this paradox has to do with some peculiar characteristics of the periods considered. The period 1950–1980 was in the majority of the countries analyzed one of very rapid population growth that, by increasing substantially the participation of school-age groups in the population, diluted the efforts that government and families made in investing in education and prevented a rapid advance of the average years of schooling in the population. Typical cases of low rates of accumulation of human capital (of around 1% per year or less, measuring human capital by years of schooling adjusted by returns to education) are Brazil (until 1980), Costa Rica (until 1970), Guatemala (until 1974), Mexico (until 1970), and Venezuela (until 1970). At the same time these are the years in which industrialization produced relatively high rates of output and productivity growth. The least successful countries in this period in terms of growth, such as Argentina and Chile in our sample, also have low rates of accumulation of human capital but they do so based on initial levels of human capital higher than the others and, having initiated the demographic transition before these and without a high population pressure, they do it at rates higher than the ones that they would record after 1980.

When several of the rapid industrialization countries entered the stage of the demographic transition characterized by low population growth rates and when the age structure of the population changed in the direction of reducing the percentage of school-age population, the rate of accumulation of human capital took off in several of them jumping to a rate of about 2% per year in Brazil (between 1980 and 2001), between 1% and 2% in Costa Rica (between 1970 and 1994), between 0.9% and 2% in Guatemala (between 1974 and 1991), and between 1.1% and 1.5% in Mexico between 1970 and 2011. But this is the period that includes the debt crisis of the 1980s that wrought havoc with the growth of GDP and TFP, followed by a disappointing growth during the post–market reform period. Where this is not happening is precisely in those countries, such as Argentina and Chile, which improved its economic performance after 1990 (in relation to the period of industrialization) and at the same time show relatively low rates of accumulation of human capital (in relation to their historical rates) in part because the benefits of the demographic bonus had already been exhausted. These interactions between demographics, human capital accumulation, and the characteristics of productive performance explain the paradox that the rate of accumulation of human capital is negatively correlated with the growth of the TFP.

Productivity Growth as an Endogenous Phenomenon

The stylized facts described in the previous section suggest the need to see productivity growth as an endogenous phenomenon and throw doubts on the explanatory power of growth accounting exercises. In particular, can and should these exercises be interpreted in causal terms, that is to attribute so much percent of the growth of output to the growth of TFP and another percent to factor accumulation? Or is the growth of productivity to a large extent endogenous, a by-product of capital accumulation and the expansion of output? This view of productivity as endogenous has been proposed by Nicholas Kaldor but its origins go back to the writings of Adam Smith and Allyn Young. Modern endogenous growth theory, starting with the papers by Romer (1986, 1990) and Lucas (1988), has brought in some of these ideas, in particular what Kaldor called dynamic economies of scale associated with learning by doing and embodied technical progress. In this section I briefly review the Kaldorian vision, which puts at the center of the growth process the presence of increasing returns to scale. I then present a simple formal analysis of this approach, which can be summarized by saying that the rate of labor productivity growth in the economy as a whole is determined by the growth rate of industrial production, the level of industrialization and the rate of expansion of the labor force.

The Smith-Young-Kaldor Tradition

In his late writings, Kaldor strongly criticized the vision of the economy based on general equilibrium and referred to the work of Adam Smith and Allyn Young as sources of alternative approaches to economic theory, in particular to the theory of economic growth (see Kaldor, 1972, 1975, 1979, 1981, 1985). In this alternative approach a crucial role is played by increasing returns, the roots of which must be found in "the nature of technological processes" (Kaldor, 1972, p. 1242).

Kaldor indicates three sources of increasing returns. The first goes back to Adam Smith and arises from the specialization and increasing division of labor made possible by the expansion of the market.[5] Indeed, in the first chapter of *The Wealth of Nations*, Adam Smith states that the income level of developed countries depends on the high degree of division of labor they attained.

Division of labor increases labor productivity, which in Smith's view is the principal factor affecting per capita income. Smith identifies three positive effects of the division of labor on workers' productivity. When workers specialize, they: (1) increase their skill (dexterity); (2) save the time necessary to switch among different activities; and (3) have the possibility of inventing machines to facilitate their job. In modern terms, we see how Smith had in mind the concepts of: (1) learning by doing; (2) setup costs; and (3) endogenous technological progress.[6]

The second source of increasing returns is related to economies of scale due to the three-dimensional nature of space. To illustrate the point, Kaldor (1972) gave the example of a pipeline: when a stretch (of unitary length) of a pipeline is constructed, the increase in output (the liquid transported) is greater than the increase in inputs (the materials used to build up the cylinder). This example was meant to represent different types of plant-level economies of scale that directly follow from an increase in production.

A third source arises from industrial specialization and division of labor and is taken directly from Young. It has to do with economies that arise from the use of specialized machines, that is, of the replacement of direct labor by indirect labor (which results in an increase in the capital–labor ratio). Young criticized Smith for his vision of the process through which specialization leads to the use of machinery, that is, more indirect methods of production[7] and he considered that the central issue is to understand when a company decides to assume the cost of a new and specialized machine either buying it or constructing it or, to put it in another way, when a company decides to use indirect labor instead of direct. In a famous passage, Young writes: "[i]n the use of machinery and the adoption of indirect processes there is a further division of labor, the economies of which are again limited by the extent of the market. It would be wasteful to make a hammer to drive a single nail,... It would be wasteful to furnish to factory with an elaborate equipment of specially constructed [machines] to build a hundred automobiles" (Young,

1928, 530). And also: "the largest advantage secured by the division of labor among industries is the fuller realizing of the economies of capitalistic or 'roundabout methods of production'" (Young, 1928, p. 539).

It is on these bases that Kaldor, in some of his late writings, developed his radical criticism of the dominant economic paradigm. In it, Kaldor criticized the traditional division between the "static" analysis of resource allocation and the "dynamic" analysis of growth as well as the analysis of growth as a result of two separate forces, factor accumulation and technical progress, a separation that becomes too artificial in the presence of increasing returns. A reallocation of resources (to or from activities with increasing returns) can, in these conditions, have a lasting impact on growth and growth itself would have to be seen as a process of structural change rather than as a mere accumulation of factors combined with technical change. After underlining the importance of increasing returns, Kaldor considered the implications for economic theory. He noted that the concept of equilibrium interpreted as an optimal allocation of resources is seriously undermined:

> [T]he whole issue, as Young said, is whether an "equilibrium of costs and advantages" is a meaningful notion in the presence of increasing returns. When every change in the use of resources- every reorganization of productive activities- creates the opportunity for a further change which would not have existed otherwise, the notion of an "optimum" allocation of resources—when every particular resource makes a great or greater contribution to output in its actual use as in any alternative use- becomes a meaningless and contradictory notion: the pattern of the use of resources at any one time can be no more than a link in the chain of an unending sequence and the very distinction, vital to equilibrium economics, between resource-creation and resource-allocation loses its validity. (Kaldor, 1975, p. 355)

In the same passage, Kaldor concludes: "[t]here can be no such thing as an equilibrium state with optimum resource allocation where no further advantageous reorganization is possible, since every such reorganization may create a fresh opportunity for a further reorganization" (Kaldor, 1975, p. 355).

In addition, as Kaldor and others used to point out, the distinction between movements along a production function and technical progress (movement of the production function) becomes blurry under increasing returns to scale. With the growth of output, more capital-intensive (or "indirect") production methods become profitable and are adopted. This happens whether these techniques were already known but not used due to the fact that they were not profitable at low levels of output, or whether they were truly new and became part of the stock of knowledge to the extent that, with the expansion of the market, the incentives for its invention appear. In developing economies, unlike those of the developed countries, these technical changes are mostly the result of the adoption of technologies from other parts. From this perspective, they constitute a movement along a production function. However, its adoption, unlike a typical movement along a production function is not the result of a change in the prices of production factors that leads to the substitution of labor for capital, but rather the result of these more capital-intensive techniques becoming profitable to the extent that the scale of the output increases.

A Kaldorian Model of Productivity Growth

How can we formalize the Kaldorian view of economic growth and aggregate productivity as a process of resource reallocation under increasing returns to scale in key sectors? Let's start by looking at the growth of aggregate labor productivity (p) as a weighted average of the productivity growth rates of two types of sectors. In Kaldor's work these are the industrial sectors (with productivity growth denoted by p_{IND}) and the non-industrial sectors (with productivity growth denoted by p_{NI}), although strictly speaking what is really important is that the first are high productivity sectors operating under increasing returns to scale and the latter are sectors of lower productivity characterized by the presence of surplus labor.

$$p = \alpha p_{IND} + \beta p_{NI} \tag{2.1}$$

In the industrial sectors, subject to increasing returns to scale, productivity growth is a function of an autonomous component (p_0) and the growth of output itself (q_{IND}). This is the so called Verdoorn law[8] that establishes, within manufacturing, a close association between the rate of labor productivity growth and the output growth rate:

$$p_{IND} = p_0 + v q_{IND} \tag{2.2}$$

Kaldor argues that in this relationship causality runs from growth of output to productivity growth as a result of the presence of increasing returns to scale in manufacturing, that is to say of static scale economies and, more importantly, dynamic ones.[9] The Verdoorn coefficient (v) is expected to be positive and less than unity, so that there is a positive relationship between employment growth and productivity growth within the industrial sector (which is important for the productivity effects of industrial growth in the nonindustrial sectors).[10]

In the nonindustrial sectors, characterized by the absence of increasing returns to scale and the presence of a labor surplus, there is no positive relationship between employment growth and productivity growth and the latter is determined so to speak "residually" as the difference between output growth and employment growth (equation 2.3). In turn, output growth is influenced by the growth of industrial production that determines the rate of increase of the flow of goods intermediated by service sectors such as wholesale and retail trade (equation 2.4). For its part, employment growth in the nonindustrial sectors results from the expansion of the labor force and the absorption of a part of this by the industrial sector (equation 2.5). So we have:

$$p_{IND} = q_{NI} - e_{NI} \quad (2.3)$$

$$q_{NI} = c0 + c1 q_{IND} \quad (2.4)$$

$$e_{NI} = (1/\psi_{NI})n - (\psi_{IND}/\psi_{NI})e_{IND} \quad (2.5)$$

Note that equation (2.5) is derived from the identity $e = \psi_{IND}$ e_{IND} + ψ_{NI} e_{NI}, where ψ_{IND} and ψ_{NI} refer to the shares in the total employment of the industrial and nonindustrial sectors, and from the assumption that $e = n$, where n is the growth of the total labor force, and e is the growth of total employment.

Thus, in addition to the prevailing mechanisms in manufacturing (Verdoorn's law), the absorption of labor force into high-productivity sectors (when these grow faster than the average) or in low-productivity sectors (when the high-productivity sectors stagnate) is another way by which the expansion of industrial production influences indirectly the overall productivity growth rate. This happens because as in industry the growth rates of output and employment are positively related, a higher rate of increase of industrial production has two consequences: (1) it leads to a greater absorption of employment in the high-productivity sectors that contributes to a reduction of the employment share of the low productivity nonindustrial sectors thereby generating productivity gains due to the reallocation of employment; (2) it reduces the rate of employment growth in the nonindustrial sectors, characterized by the absence of increasing returns to scale and the presence of surplus labor, in which the lower is the rate of employment growth, the faster will tend to be the rate of productivity growth. The higher rate of increase of the flow of goods and the reduction of informality in the low productivity nonindustrial sectors tend to raise productivity in the nonindustrial sectors. In this way, the rate of expansion of the industrial sector also influences productivity change in the nonindustrial sectors and indirectly affects the overall productivity growth rate.[11] This relationship is a

Verdoorn's law for the economy as a whole. In effect, using the above equations, we get:

$$p = f(q_{IND}, \psi_{IND}, n) \qquad f_1', f_2' > 0,\ f_3' < 0 \tag{2.6}$$

which is Kaldor's third law with the qualification that it is valid for given values of the employment share of the industrial sector and the rate of growth of the total labor force.

AN EMPIRICAL ANALYSIS OF KALDOR'S LAWS IN LATIN AMERICA

The analysis of Kaldor's laws applied to Latin American countries has antecedents in three pieces of research. Libanio (2006) provides estimations of Verdoorn's law using panel data for a sample of the seven largest Latin American economies (Argentina, Brazil, Chile, Colombia, Mexico, Peru, and Venezuela) during the period 1985–2001 using annual data from the World Development Indicators (WDI) of the World Bank. The starting point is the specification of Kaldor (1966), $e_{IND} = c + d\, q_{IND}$, where e_{IND} and q_{IND} are the employment and output growth rates in industry modified to take into account the influence of the stock of capital growth on productivity (using changes in the consumption of electricity, from WDI, as a proxy for the growth of the capital stock):

$$e_{IND} = e_0 + b\, q_{IND} + c\, k_{IND}$$

in which the degree of returns to scale is given by $(1 - c) / b$. To the extent that the stock of capital is endogenous, the author also considers a specification in which the growth of capital is endogenous:

$$tf_{IND} = d + f\, q_{IND}$$

where tf_{IND} is the rate of growth of total inputs defined as $tf_{IND} = a\, k_{IND} + (1 - a)e_{IND}$, where $(1 - a)$ is the wage share in output. Under this specification the degree of returns to scale is given by $1/f$.

Estimates of these two equations give support to Verdoorn's law in the sense that they suggest the existence of significantly increasing returns to scale in the industrial sector. The specification where k is considered as exogenous provides an estimate of returns to scale of about 1.4 and shows a low significance of the variable k. In the specification where k is treated as endogenous, the degree of returns to scale is around 2.3 with a Verdoorn coefficient of around 0.42.

Carton (2009) uses annual panel data for the period 1980–2007 for 11 countries (Argentina, Bolivia, Brazil, Chile, Colombia, Ecuador, Mexico, Paraguay, Peru, Uruguay, and Venezuela) and examines Verdoorn's law for the entire sample and for four groups according to the level of industrialization and urbanization. The data comes from the Conference Board Total Economy Database (CBTED) and Timmer and de Vries (2007). The estimations refer to an aggregate version of Verdoorn's law that relates the rate of labor productivity growth and the rate of the GDP growth for the whole economy. The results are favorable to the assumptions of increasing returns to scale and the explanatory power of the model is especially high in the group of countries with relatively high urbanization and industrialization.

Moncayo (2011) provides estimations of Kaldor's laws for the period 1950–2005 using panel data for the same sample as Libanio of the seven largest Latin American economies during the period 1950–2005. Data is annual (moving averages of five years) and comes from ECLAC and the CBTED. The estimated equations (separately for the periods 1955–1977 and 1978–2005) are:

$$q = a_0 + a_1\, q_{MAN} \qquad \text{(Kaldor's first law)}$$

$$e_{MAN} = b_0 + b_1\, q_{MAN} \qquad \text{(Verdoorn's law or Kaldor's second law)}$$

$$p = c_0 + c_1 q_{MAN} + c_2 e_{NMAN} \qquad \text{(Kaldor's third law)}$$

where e_{NMAN} is the rate of employment growth in the nonmanufacturing sectors.

The results are favorable to the three laws in the sense that the estimated coefficients are significant, and their values are in the range postulated by Kaldor.

A common difficulty in these studies is the use of annual data to investigate the long-term relationships postulated by Kaldor. For example, Verdoorn's law estimated with annual data can be confused with so-called Okun's law that postulates that productivity is pro-cyclical, that is to say that there are reasons why employment decreases less than output in recessions and increases less in booms thus making labor productivity fall in recessions and increase during booms. In what follows we will investigate Kaldor's hypotheses using rates of output growth, employment, and productivity for full economic cycles in order to capture the long-term relationships between these variables.

The information used refers to nine Latin American countries (Argentina, Bolivia, Brazil, Chile, Colombia, Costa Rica, Mexico, Peru, and Venezuela). For these nine countries we have annual data from Timmer and de Vries (2007), on value added and employment for nine sectors of economic activity from 1950 to 2005 (with the exception of Peru, which has no information for the 1950s) that was updated to 2011 with information from ECLAC and national sources. With this information and the periods defined so as to cover full economic cycles (see Appendix) we estimated growth rates of value added at constant prices (q) and employment (e) as well as, by difference, the rates of labor productivity growth ($p = q - e$).

It is worth clarifying that when testing Kaldor's hypotheses we will not deal with the multiple econometric disputes on the causal relationships between the variables involved in the equations. We only limit ourselves to examining whether the information available for the nine Latin American countries is consistent with these assumptions, without excluding other possible interpretations.

Verdoorn's Law in the Industrial Sector and Manufacturing

As mentioned before, Verdoorn's law postulates, within the manufacturing industry, a close positive association between labor productivity growth and output growth. Our estimations for the industrial and manufacturing sectors and the set of countries and time periods are:

$$p_{\text{MAN}} = 0.01 + 0.41 q_{\text{MAN}} \quad \widehat{R}^2_{(\text{adj.})} = 0.25 N = 62$$
$$(0.01)\,(4.64)$$

$$\text{With country fixed effects}: p_{\text{MAN}} = -0.06 + 0.43 q_{\text{MAN}} \quad \widehat{R}^2_{(\text{adj.})} = 0.23 N = 62$$
$$(-0.11)\,(4.49)$$

$$p_{\text{IND}} = -0.02 + 0.34 q_{\text{IND}} \quad \widehat{R}^2_{(\text{adj.})} = 0.21 N = 62$$
$$(-0.05)\,(4.10)$$

$$\text{With country fixed effects}: p_{\text{IND}} = -0.04 + 0.35 q_{\text{IND}} \quad \widehat{R}^2_{(\text{adj.})} = 0.17 N = 62$$
$$(-0.09)\,(3.88)$$

t-statistics in parentheses.

It is worth noting that the regression coefficient (the so-called Verdoorn coefficient), as postulated, in addition to being significant, is positive and less than the unity, which suggests a positive relationship between employment and productivity growth within the industrial sector.

The Relationship Between Employment and Productivity Growth in the Nonindustrial Sectors

Another component of the Kaldorian analysis is that in the nonindustrial sectors, due to the existence of diminishing returns (as in agriculture and mining) or to the presence of labor surplus (as in trade and services) the growth of employment and productivity are inversely related. This is exactly the result that we find in our set of countries as shown in Table 2.7. This table shows the estimates of regressions of the type: $p_i = a + be_i$, where p_i and e_i are the growth rates in productivity and employment in sector i.

Table 2.7 Growth in Productivity and Employment in Nonindustrial Sectors

	Constant	Regression Coefficient	$R^2_{(aj)}$
Agriculture	2.81	−0.76	0.40
	(14.40)	(−6.41)	
Mining	3.52	−0.83	0.49
	(6.75)	(−7.68)	
Commerce	1.80	−0.56	0.29
	(3.17)	(−5.09)	
Transport	3.56	−0.54	0.22
	(6.47)	(−4.23)	
Finance	1.93	−0.43	0.14
	(2.63)	(−3.31)	
Other services	1.71	−0.43	0.19
	(4.08)	(−3.91)	
Total non-industrial sectors	2.45	−0.51	0.11
	(5.31)	(−2.96)	

t-statistics in parentheses. $N = 62$.

The Growth of Production and Employment in the Nonindustrial Sectors

In the nonindustrial sectors output growth is determined by the growth of industrial production itself as it determines the rate of increase of the flow goods intermediated by service sectors such as the wholesale and retail trades. The estimate of this relationship gives the following results:

$$q_{NI} = 1.54 + 0.50\, q_{IND} \qquad \widehat{R}^2_{(adj.)} = 0.55$$
$$(5.29)\ (8.68)$$

$$\text{With fixed effects}: q_{NI} = 1.65 + 0.47\, q_{IND} \qquad \widehat{R}^2_{(adj.)} = 0.53$$
$$(5.37)\ (7.72)$$

t- statistics in parentheses. $N = 62$.

The "residual" determination of employment growth in the nonindustrial sectors implies that this growth depends positively on the expansion of the total labor force (e) and negatively on the absorption of a part of this labor force by the industrial sector (e_{IND}). The estimate of this relationship gives the following results:

$$e_{NI} = -0.01 + 1.25e - 0.24e_{IND} \qquad \widehat{R}^2_{(adj.)} = 0.99$$
$$(-0.36)\ (57.98)\ (-20.65)$$

t-statistics in parentheses. $N = 62$.

Kaldor's Third Law and Aggregate Productivity

Together, the estimated relationships above imply that labor productivity growth in the economy as a whole is a positive function of industrial output growth (that positively influences labor productivity growth in the industrial sector and indirectly labor productivity in the nonindustrial sectors through the absorption of employment from these sectors) and a negative function of total employment growth that, given the absorption of employment in the industrial sector, affects negatively labor productivity of the nonindustrial sectors by raising the rate of expansion of nonindustrial employment. The estimation of this relationship, Kaldor's third law (modified only by the inclusion of the total employment growth), gives the following results:

$$p = 1.01 + 0.62q_{IND} - 0.93e \qquad \widehat{R}^2_{(adj.)} = 0.7$$
$$(4.12)\ (13.12)\ \ (-9.83)$$

$$p = 1.04 + 0.55q_{MAN} - 0.85e \qquad \widehat{R}^2_{(adj.)} = 0.69$$
$$(3.82)\ (11.31)\ \ (-8.25)$$

t-statistics in parentheses. $N = 62$.

The estimation with country fixed effects yields very similar results. It is worth adding that the industrial employment share in total employment, contrary to what our discussion in the second section suggests, was not statistically significant when included in the above equations.

THE INTERACTIONS BETWEEN GROWTH, CAPITAL ACCUMULATION, AND PRODUCTIVITY: A SYNTHESIS AND SUMMARY

Kaldor's laws reviewed in previous sections emphasize the central role of industrial and manufacturing growth in the process of reallocation of resources, which induces and accompanies the growth of the aggregate productivity. However, they leave unanswered the question of what determines the growth of industrial production. Kaldor, of course, addressed this question in his late writings and at different times emphasized supply factors, on the one hand, and demand factors, on the other. In his analysis of the causes of slow economic growth in United Kingdom, Kaldor (1966) attributed the slow growth of manufacturing output, and therefore the slow overall economic growth, to the reduced labor supply growth available to the manufacturing sector, resulting from a "premature maturity" of the British economy that would have exhausted prematurely its surplus of labor in the nonindustrial sectors. In later writings both he and Thirlwall, based on Kaldor's writing, emphasized demand constraints associated with the income elasticity of exports and imports that given global growth would determine jointly the growth of manufacturing production and, through the mechanisms described, the overall rate of economic growth (see, for the most recent version of this hypothesis, Pacheco-López and Thirlwall, 2013).

There is another possible response that allows us to reconcile Kaldor's late writings, with his emphasis on industrial growth, with his earlier writings on growth theory and his emphasis on capital accumulation. This synthesis and reconciliation starts from the recognition that in very open developing economies the constraints on demand determined by the balance of payments stop playing the central role that they could have had in the past when these economies grew on the basis of the domestic market and, with a fixed exchange rate, macroeconomic policy had to maintain aggregate demand within the limits allowed by the state of the balance of payments. Under the conditions that have been generated by trade openness, the larger role of foreign trade and the transition to flexible exchange rate regimes, the growth of manufacturing output, the traded goods sector par excellence, is largely determined by the rate of capital accumulation that determines the growth of the productive capacity in those tradable sectors. By viewing in this way the determinants of industrial expansion we are able to link Kaldor's hypotheses to his earlier writings based on his technical progress function, according to which the rate at which output per worker grows is a function of the rate at which capital per worker increases. This is because, to paraphrase the author, the technical innovations that increase the productivity of labor usually require the use of more capital per worker and also because the rate at which an economy can absorb the inventions and innovations of the past that are still unexploited is limited by its rate of capital accumulation. In the synthesis that we are proposing these mechanisms should be added to those derived from the presence of increasing returns to scale in the industrial sector and the productivity gains associated with the reallocation of resources toward this sector.

Thus, if we combine Kaldor's third law $p = f(q_{\mathrm{IND}}, e)$, with the determination of the growth of industrial production by the rate of capital accumulation, $q_{\mathrm{IND}} = g(I/K)$, we get:

$$p = F(I/K, e) \quad (2.7)$$

Equation (2.7) is a version of Kaldor's technical progress function, which, however, we should now interpret taking into account not only the endogeneity of technical progress but also the mechanisms through which the reallocation of resources toward the industrial sector promotes the growth of labor productivity in both industrial and nonindustrial sectors.

This synthesis, of course, generates new questions: how is the rate of capital accumulation determined? This question leads us to the neo-Keynesian literature on economic growth, which sees the rate of capital accumulation as depending on profitability, in turn determined by the degree of capacity utilization and the profit markup (see Dutt, 1984; Bhaduri and Marglin, 1990). In the case of an open developing economy, the markup in tradable goods sectors is decisively related to the real exchange rate so that we can postulate the determination of the rate of capital accumulation as:

$$I / K = G(u, rer, p)$$

where u is the degree of productive capacity utilization, *rer* is the real exchange rate, and p is the rate of growth of aggregate productivity that reflects the positive effect of productivity gains on the rate of accumulation in both industrial and nonindustrial sectors (to the extent, e.g., that the reduction of labor surplus in nonindustrial sectors stimulates the accumulation of capital there).

Figure 2.1 shows the simultaneous determination of the rates of productivity growth and capital accumulation assuming that the effect of capital accumulation on productivity is stronger than the effect of productivity growth on the rate of capital accumulation.

Increases in the degree of utilization and the real exchange rate move outward the accumulation line leading to increases in the rate of accumulation and productivity growth. Increases in

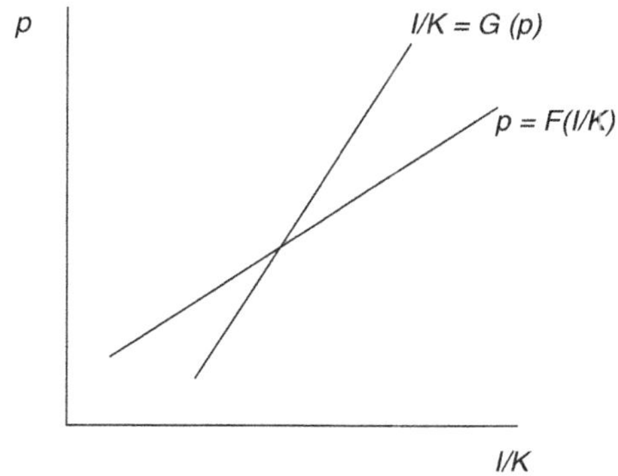

Figure 2.1 Simultaneous Determination of Capital Accumulation and Productivity Growth

labor force growth move down the productivity line and reduce both the rate of productivity growth and the rate of capital accumulation.

In other chapters of this book some of the determinants of capital accumulation are examined. What we can conclude at this point is that, contrary to the exercises of growth accounting that postulate the exogeneity of TFP, the dependence of productivity growth on capital accumulation per worker and the evidence in favor of the Kaldorian hypotheses clearly suggest that the slowdown in TFP growth in the last 30 years in Latin America is endogenous to the loss of dynamism of the overall process of economic growth and the slowdown of physical capital accumulation. Nothing illustrates more dramatically this endogeneity than the lost decade of the eighties during which growth stopped due to the demand constraints imposed by the debt crisis and external credit rationing, capital accumulation collapsed, and with it productivity growth fell in the industrial sectors and, through growing informality in the labor market, also in the trade and services sectors, bringing with it a collapse of aggregate labor productivity and TFP.

APPENDIX

Statistical Information

The selection of countries covers large, small, and medium economies of Latin America for which there are internationally comparable data on the stock of capital and aggregate employment and by sectors. These series of value-added, capital, and employment are indispensable in order to estimate TFP and test different hypotheses about the relationship between productivity, capital accumulation, and growth. The Penn World Table (PWT) 8.0 provides information about these aggregates for 11 Latin American countries from 1950 to 2011: Argentina, Bolivia, Brazil, Chile, Colombia, Costa Rica, Ecuador, Guatemala, Mexico, Peru, and Venezuela. In addition, information on value added and employment by sector is used.

Timmer and de Vries (2007) have estimates of value added and employment for nine sectors of economic activity (agriculture, mining, manufacturing, electricity, gas and water, construction, trade, transport and communications, financial services, insurance and real estate, and community, social and personal services) and nine Latin American countries (the previous 11 minus Ecuador and Guatemala). These estimates refer to the period 1950–2005 and were updated to 2011 using national and international sources. In some exercises the sectors were aggregated into industrial (manufacturing industry, electricity, gas and water, and construction) and nonindustrial (the rest).

The Selection of Time Periods

The measurement of growth rates refers to periods that include complete economic cycles or, more precisely, those whose initial and final year were in similar stages of the cycle. In this way, the selection of the periods was based on the principle of choosing years where the degree of utilization of productive capacity reaches a peak, with the aim of capturing in each period medium and long-term trends. As an approximation to the degree of utilization TFP from 1950 to 2011 along with the GDP series were used. The definition of the periods in this manner removes biases in the estimation of output, employment, labor productivity, and TFP derived from a different degree of utilization of productive factors in the initial and final years of each period.

In this exercise, TFP was calculated as $\log TFP = \log GDP - \alpha \log K - (1 - \alpha) \log(Lh)$ where log is the natural logarithm, GDP is GDP at national constant prices of 2005 (RGDPNA in the PWT 8.0), K is the stock of capital at national constant prices of 2005 (RKNA), L is employment measured in number of workers (EMP), and h are the average hours worked per person (AVH). When the latter were not available the number of workers was used to measure employment. The coefficients α and $(1 - \alpha)$ are, respectively, the capital and wage shares in GDP at current national prices (1 – LABSH and LABSH in PWT 8.0).

The original series of the logarithm of TFP were smoothed with a Hodrick-Prescott filter ($\lambda = 100$) in order to capture long-term trends. It was estimated then, for each country, the difference between the values of the original and the filtered series and "peak years" were identified when the difference between the two series reaches a local maximum. More precisely, a "peak year" is defined as a year in which the difference between the value of the original series of TFP and the filtered series is moving upward and reaches a value higher than the previous two years as well as to the following two years. One restriction is that the periods thus identified must have a minimum of five years.[12]

The periods obtained are the following:

Argentina: 1951–1960, 1960–1969, 1969–1974, 1974–1980, 1980–1987, 1987–1998, 1998–2008
Bolivia: 1952–1957, 1957–1967, 1967–1975, 1975–1989, 1989–1996, 1996–2001, 2001–2009
Brazil: 1952–1961, 1961–1974, 1974–1980, 1980–1987, 1987–1995, 1995–2001, 2001–2008
Chile: 1953–1960, 1960–1966, 1966–1971, 1971–1981, 1981–1992, 1992–1998, 1998–2007
Colombia: 1954–1961, 1961–1974, 1974–1980, 1980–1989, 1989–1997, 1997–2007
Costa Rica: 1955–1960, 1960–1970, 1970–1979, 1979–1986, 1986–1994, 1994–2002, 2002–2011
Ecuador: 1954–1964, 1964–1973, 1973–1981, 1981–1988, 1988–1998, 1998–2008
Guatemala: 1950–1956, 1956–1963, 1963–1968, 1968–1974, 1974–1980, 1980–1991, 1991–2001, 2001–2006, 2006–2011
Mexico: 1951–1957, 1957–1964, 1964–1970, 1970–1981, 1981–1994, 1994–2000, 2000–2011
Peru: 1954–1962, 1962–1971, 1971–1981, 1981–1987, 1987–1997, 1997–2003, 2003–2008
Venezuela: 1952–1957, 1957–1964, 1964–1970, 1970–1976, 1976–1981, 1981–1992, 1992–1998, 1998–2008

3

The Real Exchange Rate, the Real Wage, and Growth: A Formal Analysis of the "Development Channel"*

Traditional macroeconomic analysis suggests that a higher real exchange rate (RER) has a positive effect on the balance of payments constrained *level* of economic activity provided, of course, that the Marshall–Lerner condition is fulfilled. This is the traditional "macroeconomic channel": a higher RER enhances competitiveness of exports and raises import prices thus strengthening the competitiveness of import-competing local producers. In so doing it improves the trade balance and the level of output corresponding to a given trade deficit. A recent, mostly empirical, literature suggests the existence of a *growth*, rather than *level*, effect on output of a higher RER. Indeed, the relationship between the RER and the rate of economic growth has been receiving a great deal of attention in recent times after the extraordinarily high growth rates achieved by countries that have deliberately undervalued their RERs and the slow growth rates experienced by a large number of countries with overvalued exchange rates. The first case is illustrated with the experience of China (see Razmi, Rapetti, and Skott, 2012) and, in the Latin American context and to a lesser extent, of Argentina, while the second case can be illustrated with the experience of Mexico (see Blecker, 2009; Ibarra, 2010; Moreno-Brid and Ros, 2009). This relationship has been the object of a large and increasing number of empirical studies and significantly less theoretical discussion.

One aim of this chapter is to contribute to an understanding of how and why the RER may affect long-run growth. For this, the chapter relies on the "development channel" highlighted in Frenkel and Ros (2006) in the analysis of the relationship between the RER and employment in Latin America. This channel is implicitly or explicitly present in both writings of Béla Balassa (1971) and Nicholas Kaldor (1971) and their advocacy of export-led growth (see Frenkel and Ros, 2006). Another aim is to clarify the short- and long-run relationships between the RER and the real wage. Almost inevitably a higher RER implies a lower real wage in the short run. At the same time, by promoting investment in sectors where productivity increases endogenously with output and capital accumulation, a higher RER may imply a higher real wage in the long run. And vice versa for a real exchange appreciation: Krugman (1987) and Ros and Skott (1998) discuss how a transitorily higher real wage resulting from a RER appreciation can lead to a permanent long-run reduction of the real wage in the presence of dynamic economies of scale.

The chapter is organized as follows. The first section reviews the empirical studies showing a relationship between exchange rate misalignment and slow growth and between undervaluation and fast growth and the suggested explanations of these relationships. The second section presents the basic assumptions of the analytical framework. The third section discusses the interactions between profitability and capital accumulation in the medium and long term in the absence of technical progress. The fourth section extends the analysis to the case of endogenous technical progress drawing on the contributions of Nicholas Kaldor and Joan Robinson to the theory of economic growth. In this framework a depreciated RER contributes to a higher level of employment and higher real wages in the long run and, under certain conditions, to faster long-term growth through its effects on the profitability of investment. The key necessary condition refers the presence of increasing returns to scale in the traded goods sector. A final section concludes.

EMPIRICAL FINDINGS AND SUGGESTED MECHANISMS

By now there are many empirical studies that find negative correlations between exchange rate misalignment and growth—the more overvalued the currency, the lower the per capita growth rate—or positive correlations between undervaluation and its correlates, on one hand, and growth, on the other. Cavallo et al. (1990) present cross-country regressions among developing countries for the period 1960–1983 showing a negative correlation between per capita GDP growth and a measure of (policy induced) misalignment of the RER, as well as a measure of RER instability. Dollar (1992) finds a significant, negative relationship between distortion in the RER and per capita GDP growth over the period 1976–1985 for a group of developing countries after controlling for the effects of RER variability and level of investment. Thus, for example, African countries with the highest degree of overvaluation are the slowest growing and Asian countries with the lowest degree of distortion are the fastest growing (with Latin American countries falling in between). Razin and Collins (1997) find nonlinearities in the relationship between misalignment and growth: only very high overvaluations appear to be associated with slower growth while moderate to high (but not very high undervaluations) are associated with high growth. The analysis refers to 93 countries over the period 1975 to 1992 and controls for a number of indicators of initial conditions, external environment, and macroeconomic policy. The estimates imply that a 10% overvaluation is associated with a decline in real per capita GDP growth of 0.6 percentage points. Polterovich and Popov (2002) present cross-country regressions showing that the rapid accumulation of foreign exchange reserves, associated with policies intended to sustain depreciated exchange rates, leads to export-led growth. Countries with rapidly growing foreign exchange reserves to GDP ratios exhibit higher investment/GDP ratios, higher trade/GDP ratios, higher capital productivity, and higher rates of growth. Acemoglu et al. (2003) find that overvaluation of the RER is the only macroeconomic variable (the others being government consumption and the average rate of inflation) that has a negative effect on growth after controlling for institutional variables and initial GDP per capita over the period 1970–1998. Prasad et al. (2007) show with a wide sample of developing countries between 1970 and 2004 a positive association between growth rates and current accounts in the balance of payments (even after controlling for standard determinants of growth) and between growth and RERs. In terms of magnitude, their results suggest that in the short run a 1 percentage point increase in the degree of overvaluation accompanies a decline in growth of about 0.4 percentage point. Overvaluation is measured as the deviation of the exchange rate from purchasing power parity after accounting for differences in incomes (Balassa–Samuelson effect). Levy-Yeyati and Sturzenegger (2007) find that there is an effect of exchange rate intervention on growth, that is, depreciated exchange rates appear to induce higher growth. Gala (2008) uses a panel of 58 developing countries in the period from 1960 to 1999 and shows a negative association between overvaluation and per capita GDP growth after controlling for initial level of income and structural and macroeconomic characteristics. The estimates imply that a 10% undervaluation is associated with a per capita GDP growth up to 0.15% higher. Rodrik (2008) reaches similar results for a sample of 184 countries and finds that the link between undervaluation and growth is particularly strong among developing countries. Razmi, Rapetti, and Skott (2012) find a positive effect of the RER on investment growth, especially among developing countries, in the period 1960–2004. They confirm these results and show that the effects of currency undervaluation on growth are larger and more robust in developing economies.

There are a number of suggested mechanisms through which the RER influences growth. Ros and Skott (1998) emphasize the profitability effects of the RER on capital accumulation. In the presence of increasing returns to scale in the traded goods sector, the profitability squeeze produced by overvaluation can lead the economy to a lower-level equilibrium following a period of contraction and falling real wages. Similarly, Polterovich and Popov (2002) point to the positive effects on investment of the higher profitability in the traded goods sectors. The impact of investment on growth is amplified by the higher productivity of the invested capital, mostly in sectors subject to international competition. Frenkel (2004) and Frenkel and Ros (2006) highlight the "development channel" operating through the profitability and expansion of the traded goods sector as the development of tradable activities generates specialization economies and learning externalities that are capitalized by less dynamic sectors. Gala (2008) also highlights the profitability channel, as well as the role of technological change, in the context of a neo-Keynesian model of profit-led growth. Rodrik (2008) emphasizes the expansion of the traded goods sector viewing a depreciated RER as a second best policy that helps overcome the institutional and market failures that particularly affect that sector. Razmi, Rapetti, and Skott (2012) view the real exchange as an instrument to reconcile a sustainable trade balance with a target rate of accumulation: given a target for the trade balance, a real depreciation is required to achieve a higher rate of accumulation in order to switch domestic expenditure away from tradable goods and allow for increased capital good imports necessary a for a higher investment. A similar mechanism is present in the balance of payments constrained growth model of Porcile and Lima (2010). By contrast, Levy-Yeyati and Sturzenegger (2007) argue that the effect, rather than through a boost to the tradable goods sector via import substitution or export growth, works largely through the increase of domestic savings. Devaluation, as in Díaz-Alejandro (1965) classical analysis, redistributes income from low-income, low-saving propensity workers to high-income capitalists. This boosts overall savings. In small and medium firms with limited access to finance, this increases internal funds with a positive effect on investment. The increase in overall savings also tends to lower the cost of capital for large companies that fund their investments in capital markets.

A Small Open-Economy Model: The Basic Assumptions

The economy considered produces a single tradable good and firms face given terms of trade in international markets and are also price takers in the domestic market. This small open economy assumption is, in my view, an appropriate analytical framework for the typical developing economy whose growth leaves by and large unaffected the terms of trade that it faces in international markets.

Firms maximize profits equal to $PY - WL$, where P is the domestic price equal to the international price times a constant nominal exchange rate equal to one, W is the nominal wage, Y is output, and L is labor input. Firms maximize profits, taking nominal wages and prices as given, subject to a production function constraint $Y = F(A, K, L)$ where K is capital input. The level of productivity (A) is, for the time being, taken as exogenously given and constant over time. From the first-order condition for profit maximization, we have the equality between the real wage and the marginal product of labor:

$$W/P = F'(L) \tag{3.1}$$

The determination of employment is derived from equation (3.1). Indeed, solving (3.1) for L yields: $L = L(A, W/P, K)$, which shows the level of employment determined by the capital stock, the real wage, and the level of productivity with L_A, $L_K > 0$ and $L_{W/P} < 0$. This level of employment (and output) is therefore independent of domestic demand. Firms do not increase production in response to higher domestic demand (given the real wage, W/P). Rather, they adjust by reducing exports and increasing sales in the domestic market. The reason is that they face a perfectly elastic demand for exports. Indeed, if they increased production in response to higher domestic demand, their marginal cost would increase above the price of exports. This would induce them to reduce their exports until the marginal cost of production is again equal to the price of exports. This means that a higher domestic demand fully crowds out exports. A higher level of foreign demand, by contrast, to the extent that it increases the international price of exports has a positive effect on employment and output given the nominal wage. The same effect results from a devaluation of the nominal exchange rate since it increases domestic and export prices in domestic currency.

With respect to the demand side, we assume there are no savings out of wages and let s_p be the propensity to save out profits. Consumption (C) is then determined as: $PC = WL + (1 - s_p)(PY - WL)$, where we are assuming away, for simplicity, imports of consumption goods. Investment has a domestic (I_d) and an imported component (M_k). Thus: $P_I I = PI_d + P_M M_k$, where P_I is the price of capital goods and $M_k = mI$, so that there is a fixed amount ($m < 1$) of complementary imports per unit of total investment.

INTERACTIONS BETWEEN PROFITABILITY AND ACCUMULATION IN THE MEDIUM AND LONG TERM

We now derive two relationships between the profit rate and the rate of accumulation such that, in a steady state, profit expectations are fulfilled and the rates of growth of output and the capital stock are constant and, as we shall see below, equal to

Robinson's "desired rate of accumulation" (Robinson, 1962). Note, first, that combining the definition of the profit rate with equation (3.1) implies:

$$r = a\,(P/P_I)\,u \qquad u = u(A,\ W/P) \qquad u_A > 0,\ u_{W/P} < 0 \tag{3.2}$$

where a is the profit share in output (assumed constant) and u is the output-capital ratio (Y/K). The profit rate is thus a decreasing function of the real wage and of the ratio of capital goods prices to export prices, P_I/P, that is, an increasing function of the country's terms of trade, and is independent of the rate of accumulation (g).[1] Equation (3.2) is thus the equation of a horizontal line in Figure 3.1 in (r, g) space.[2]

The second relationship is a rate of accumulation function that makes the rate of accumulation depend on the propensity to invest (b) and the expected profit rate (r^e) (a la Joan Robinson, 1962), as well as a risk-adjusted international profit rate (r^*):

$$g = b\,(r^e - r^*) \quad \text{(which implies with } r = r^e, \quad r = (g/b) + r^*\text{)} \tag{3.3}$$

In a steady state, $r^e = r$. Figure 3.1 shows the determination of the steady state values of g and r. At the intersection of the two lines, corresponding to equations (3.2) and (3.3), the rate of accumulation generates a profit rate that just equals the expected profit rate that induced this rate of accumulation.[3] This desired or equilibrium rate of accumulation is analogous to Harrod's warranted growth rate. For, in the present open economy context, it is such that the investment forthcoming at the equilibrium profit rate generates an addition to productive capacity such that the increase in domestic demand leaves the composition of total output between exports and domestic sales unchanged. Thus, on the warranted growth path, exports and domestic demand grow at the same rate, equal to the rate of growth of productive capacity.

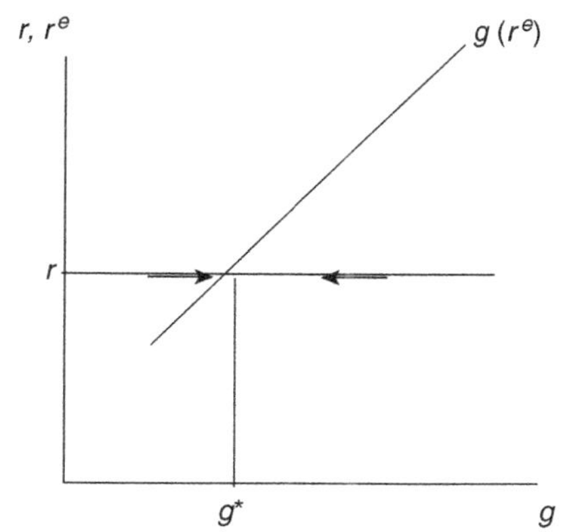

Figure 3.1 The Warranted Growth Rate.

Short- and Long-Run Effects of a Real Devaluation in the Absence of Technical Progress

Above the $g(r^e)$ line (given by equation 3.3), the profit rate is higher than expected and investment decisions will be revised upward, while below the line the rate of profit is lower than expected and the rate of accumulation decreases. With continuous market clearing in the goods market, and in the absence of labor supply constraints, the economy converges through the r line to the stable equilibrium at the intersection of the r line and the $g(r^e)$ line.

Consider the effects of a devaluation of the RER (a higher P/W). This shifts the r line up, moving the economy to a new equilibrium path with a higher growth rate and a lower real wage.[4] The increase in growth holds however only for a short- or medium-run period in which we can neglect changes in nominal wages. In order to examine what happens beyond this short period, we have to consider the adjustment of nominal wages and the RER that will occur as a consequence of labor market conditions.

Consider, first, the determinants of the rate of wage inflation. We adopt here a structuralist specification that makes the growth rate of nominal wages (w) depend on the rate of domestic price inflation (p) and the gap between a target (or bargained) real wage (ω) and the real consumption wage effectively received by workers (W/P):

$$w = p + \lambda\,(\omega - W/P) \qquad \omega = \omega\,(L/N)\ \omega' > 0 \qquad (3.4)$$

Further, we assume that the target real wage is an inverse function of the unemployment rate (i.e., an increasing function of the employment rate, L/N, where N is the total labor force). This inverse relationship is supported by empirical research on the "wage curve," which establishes a negative relationship across regions and sectors between wage levels and unemployment (see Blanchflower and Oswald, 1994, 2005). The wage inflation equation is thus similar to a Phillips curve equation augmented by the effects of expected price inflation. Indeed, as long as the nominal exchange rate is constant and foreign inflation is zero, current price inflation is nil and current inflation coincides with expected inflation. Equation (3.4) can also be interpreted as showing the dynamic behavior of the real consumption wage, $w - p$, as an inverse function of its level: a higher real wage implies a slower growth of nominal wages in relation to domestic prices. The feedback effect on the growth of the real wage is negative and thus stabilizing.

Consider now the dynamic behavior of the employment rate over time. Assuming a Cobb–Douglas production function $Y = AK^{a} L^{1-a}$, and solving (3.1) for the level of employment (L), yields: $L = [A\,(1 - a)/(W/P)]^{1/a}\,K$. Taking logs in this employment equation and differentiating with respect to time, and then subtracting the rate of growth of the labor force (n) from both sides of the equation, we have:

$$l - n = g - (1/a)\,(w - p) - n \quad g = g\,(W/P) \quad g' < 0 \qquad (3.5)$$

where l is the rate of growth of employment and p is the rate of price inflation. In equation (3.5), g, the rate of capital accumulation, equal to the rate of growth of the capital stock assuming no depreciation of capital, is determined by equations (3.2) and (3.3) under the assumption $r = r^*$. We express this equilibrium rate of accumulation as an inverse function of the real wage. Other variables and parameters affecting the equilibrium rate of accumulation are the propensity to invest, the level of productivity and the risk adjusted international profit rate. Note that since the growth of the real wage in equation (3.4) is an increasing function of the employment rate, equation (3.5) shows the rate of change of the employment rate $(l - n)$ as an inverse function of its level.

Consider now the dynamic adjustments in real wages and the employment rate. Setting $w = p$ in (4), we obtain the equation of a locus of $(L/N, W/P)$ combinations along which the real wage is stationary:

$$\lambda\,(\omega\,(L/N) - W/P) = 0$$

In $(L/N, W/P)$ space, this is an upward sloping schedule: a higher employment rate tends to raise w above p and this requires a higher real wage, which reduces w, in order to maintain stability of the real wage. Because the feedback effect of the real wage on its rate of change is negative (and thus stabilizing), the real wage falls when above the locus and increases when below it (see Figure 3.2). The position of the schedule is determined by labor market parameters (the $\omega\,(\cdot)$ function).

Substituting from (4) into (5) and setting $l = n$, we obtain a locus of $(L/N, W/P)$ combinations along which the employment rate is stationary:

$$g\,(W/P) - (1/a)\,\lambda\,[\omega\,(L/N) - W/P)] - n = 0 \quad g' < 0 \quad \omega' > 0$$

This schedule can have a negative or a positive slope. The reason is that a higher real wage has two effects on the rate of growth of employment. First, it reduces employment growth through its negative effect on the rate of accumulation. Second, it increases employment growth through its negative effect on

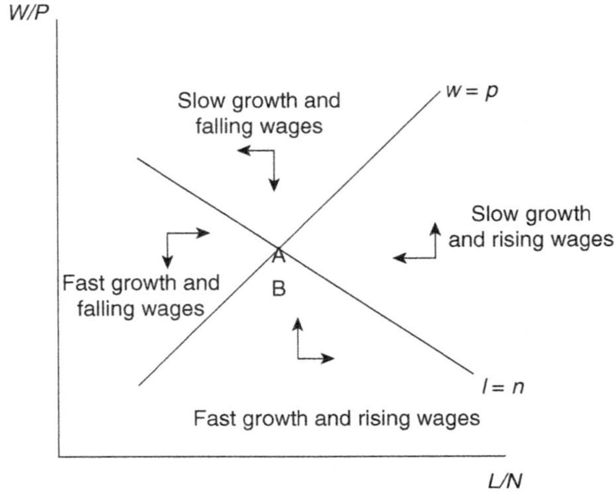

Figure 3.2 Long-term Dynamic Adjustments.

the growth of real wages. In Figure 3.2, I assume that the first effect is stronger than the second and this is why the schedule is downward sloping: the negative effect on employment growth of a higher real wage requires a lower employment rate (which by reducing wage growth increases employment growth) in order to keep the employment rate stable (see appendix for further analysis). The position of the schedule is determined by parameters, such as the propensity to invest, affecting the $g(\cdot)$ function, and labor market parameters affecting the $\lambda(\cdot)$ and $\omega(\cdot)$ functions. Because the feedback effect of the employment rate on its growth (given by $l - n$) is stabilizing, the employment rate increases when the economy is to the right of the schedule and falls when it is to the left.

The two schedules of real wage and employment stability divide the $(W/P, L/N)$ space into four regions as depicted in Figure 3.2. As shown in the diagram, provided that the long-run equilibrium at the intersection of the two schedules is stable, the economy converges to a steady state in which the rate of capital accumulation is equal to Harrod's natural rate (the growth rate of the labor force, n, under our present assumptions) while the output-capital ratio, the employment rate, the RER, and real wages all remain constant over time. The appendix discusses the stability conditions.

It is clear from this analysis that the short-run effects of a devaluation on growth and real wages will be reversed in the long run under our present assumptions. Consider indeed in Figure 3.2 the effects of a devaluation starting from a long-run equilibrium at point *A* with $g = n$. The economy moves to point *B* in the short run into the region of increasing employment and rising wages. The gains in employment are, however, short term and reversible since they are eventually offset by higher wages that make the economy converge, through oscillations, to the initial long-term equilibrium at point *A*, in which the rate of capital accumulation is equal to the natural rate and real wages and the RER are equal to their initial values.

LONG-RUN EFFECTS OF A REAL DEVALUATION IN THE PRESENCE OF ENDOGENOUS TECHNICAL PROGRESS

We now extend the model to consider changes in productivity (A). Note that these changes will now affect labor demand, the output-capital ratio, and the rate of profit, all of which are increasing functions of A. The evolution of A over time responds to a productivity growth function (or "technical progress function" in Kaldor's terminology), which is based on the contributions of Nicholas Kaldor and Joan Robinson to the theory of economic growth. As discussed in chapter 2, Kaldor indicates three sources of increasing returns. The first, of a static nature, are the economies of scale due to the three-dimensional nature of space. The other two sources refer to two aspects of specialization: the substitution of direct for indirect labor (i.e., an increase in the capital/labor ratio), and learning by doing, a source of technological externalities.[5] As a result of the last two aspects, in Kaldor's view (1957) productivity increases are endogenous to the process of capital accumulation per worker.

For Joan Robinson, productivity growth is influenced by labor and goods market conditions. Firms speed up the diffusion of new technologies in response to shortages in the labor market by adopting new techniques which reduce labor costs.[6] As she puts it: "[e]ven more important than speeding up discoveries is the speeding up of the rate at which innovations are diffused. When entrepreneurs find themselves in a situation where potential markets are expanding but labour hard to find, they have every motive to increase productivity" (Robinson (1956, p. 96).

We put together these ideas by assuming the following productivity growth function:

$$\rho = \mu\,(g - l) + \psi\,(l - n) \tag{3.6}$$

which makes the rate of productivity growth (ρ) a function of the rate of growth of the capital labor ratio ($g - l$, a la Kaldor) and the excess of employment growth over the growth of the labor force ($l - n$, a la Robinson).

In Kaldor's and Robinson's views, technical change has a strong element of irreversibility. That is what Kaldor meant by "dynamic" in the expression "dynamic economies of scale." If this is the case, in equation (3.9) $\mu\,(g - l) = 0$ if $g < l$, and $\psi\,(l - n) = 0$ if $l < n$. We shall consider also the case of reversible productivity changes in which equation (3.6) holds without restrictions.

A second change is that we modify the wage inflation equation as follows. We assume as before that the target real wage is determined by labor market conditions (the employment rate, L/N). But, in order to simplify the analysis and clarify the processes of adjustment, I assume that nominal wages growth differs from the rate of domestic inflation only when the target wage is above the actual real wage. Otherwise, that is, if the real consumption wage is above the target real wage, nominal wages grow exactly at the rate of price inflation (and not below it). The target real wage is then really a threshold that triggers wage inflation (above price inflation) only when the actual wage falls below it (for a similar specification, see Basu's formalization of Kalecki's model of inflation in Basu, 1997). Equation (3.4) is thus replaced by:

$$w = p + \lambda(\omega - W/P) \quad \omega = \omega(L/N),\ \omega' > 0 \quad \text{for } \omega > W/P$$
$$w = p \qquad \text{for } \omega \leq W/P \quad (3.7)$$

Consider now, under the present assumptions, the effects of a devaluation starting from an initial long-term equilibrium at point *A* in Figures 3.3 and 3.4. Suppose that the initial employment rate is so low that the real wage is above the threshold wage so that nominal wages are constant (since with the given nominal exchange rate, domestic inflation is nil). Thus, the economy is on a warranted path that is also a long-term equilibrium with $g = l$ and $l = n$. K/L and L/N are thus also constant. Since then $\rho = 0$, at this equilibrium the level of productivity is also constant.

Now suppose that the price level increases as a result of a devaluation. The real wage falls and the r line shifts upward. The profit rate and the rate of accumulation increase toward a new warranted path at point *B*. Since the rate of accumulation

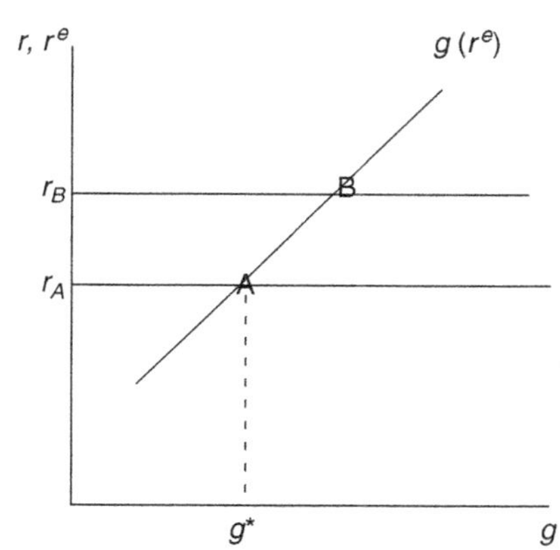

Figure 3.3 Short- and Long-term Effects of a Real Devaluation.

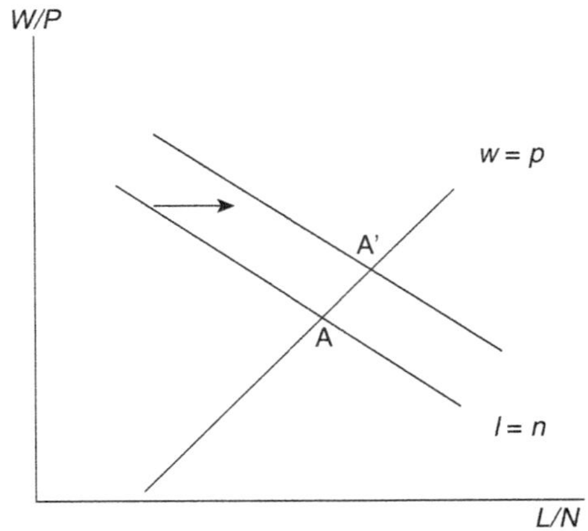

Figure 3.4 Long-term Dynamic Adjustments with Irreversible Productivity Changes.

increases, employment growth increases above the growth of the labor force. The employment rate increases but the capital labor ratio falls (as a result of the positive employment effect of the fall in the product wage). Suppose that initially nominal wages do not change because although the real wage falls as a consequence of devaluation it remains above the threshold wage given the initially very low employment rate (this will be true, of course, provided that the devaluation is not so large as to reduce the real wage below the threshold). In the new warranted path, the employment rate is increasing and through its effect on productivity the *r* line will keep on shifting up toward a still higher warranted growth rate.[7]

There will come a point, at a sufficiently high employment rate, in which the threshold wage will become higher than the real wage. At this point, nominal and real wages start increasing, bringing about a fall in the rates of profit and capital accumulation. Employment growth therefore falls as a result of both the fall in the rate of capital accumulation and the positive growth of wages. This process brings employment growth back into equality with the growth of the labor force. At the point in which employment growth is again equal to the growth of the labor force, the employment rate stops increasing. However, at this higher employment rate, nominal wages may (or may not) continue to grow. There are several possibilities.

Suppose that wages continue to grow because at the employment rate considered the target wage is above the real wage. As wages increase, the growth of employment falls below the growth of the labor force causing the employment rate to fall. The target wage thus falls until wage growth is again zero. If at this point the rates of capital accumulation and employment growth are lower than the rate of labor force growth, the employment rate continues to fall. With reversible productivity changes, productivity falls and it is conceivable that the resulting fall in the profit rate brings the economy back to point *A*. In terms of the diagram in $(L/N,\ W/P)$ space, the shifts in the schedule of employment stability that took place as a result of the changes in productivity are completely reversed and the economy goes back to the initial long-run equilibrium.

A second possibility is that when wage growth falls back to zero, the employment rate stabilizes at a higher level than the initial one. In this case, the economy will converge to a long-run equilibrium which features the same rates of profit and capital accumulation than the initial equilibrium (the economy goes back to point *A* in Figure 3.3) but at higher levels of productivity, the capital–labor ratio and the employment rate, all of which increased during the process of adjustment. In terms of Figure 3.4, the higher level of productivity shifts the schedule of employment stability to the right and the economy converges to a new long-run equilibrium at point A' with a higher employment rate and a higher real wage (since productivity and the capital–labor ratio are higher than their initial values, it is easily verified from the labor demand function that the real wage, W/P, is higher). So, even with reversible productivity changes it is possible for the devaluation to have positive long-term effects on real wages and the employment rate. In this case, what prevents the return to the initial long-term equilibrium at point *A* is the fact that nominal wages do not fall once the threshold wage is brought back below the actual wage and therefore the capital–labor ratio (and the level of productivity) do not continue to fall.

With irreversible productivity changes, the technical changes and new technologies introduced as a result of the increase in the employment rate following the devaluation and the increase in the rates of profit and capital accumulation will unambiguously shift the schedule of employment stability to the right as a result of the increase in the level of productivity during the adjustment process. This leads the economy to a new long-run equilibrium at A' in Figure 3.4 with a higher employment rate and higher real wages. In Figure 3.3, in (r, g) space, the $r(g)$ line shifts back to its initial position as a result of the increase in real wages.

What if the target wage is an increasing function of the level of productivity? Suppose equation (3.7) is replaced by:

$$w = p + \lambda\,(\omega - W/P) \quad \omega = \omega\,(L/N, A), \quad \omega_1, \omega_2 > 0, \quad \text{for } \omega > W/P$$
$$w = p \quad \text{for } \omega \leq W/P \qquad (3.7')$$

A real devaluation can now have a long-term growth effect. In this case, wages do not stabilize as the employment rate falls and reduces the target wage. Rather, it is possible that the negative effect of wage growth on employment growth is compensated by a higher rate of capital accumulation resulting from the higher profit rate. At the same time, the negative effect of wage increases on the profit rate is compensated by the positive effect on productivity growth of the rate of accumulation being higher than employment growth (precisely because wage growth is positive). The economy then converges to a new long-term equilibrium with a rate of capital accumulation higher than the growth of employment and a positive rate of growth of wages. It is a long-term equilibrium, which, compared to the initial one, features a higher rate of accumulation and faster growth of real wages, faster productivity growth, and a constant employment rate. Unlike what happens in the previous cases, as productivity increases over time the target wage keeps on increasing, continually disturbing the equality with actual wages and causing the latter to grow over time. In $(L/N, W/P)$ space, the shifts to the right of the schedule of employment stability are accompanied by upward shifts of the schedule of wage stability, which keep the employment rate constant and real wages increasing. In (r, g) space, the economy converges to a warranted path in which the rate of capital accumulation is higher than the rate of growth of the labor force and output per worker is continually increasing as a result of productivity growth equal to $\rho = \mu (g - l)$. Thus, on the long-run equilibrium path the economy no longer grows at the rate of growth of the labor force. The output growth rate is no longer exogenous; it is equal to $(\mu + a) g + (1 - a - \mu)$ n and that of output per worker is $(\mu + a)(g - n)$, where g is the warranted growth rate that is constrained by the propensity to invest. The warranted rate of capital accumulation is now a determinant of the natural rate.

CONCLUSIONS

The models presented in this chapter aim at giving a theoretical foundation to the "profitability" or "development" channel postulated in the empirical literature on the RER and growth. They also aim to answer the question of what happens with the long-run effects of a real devaluation on real wages in the presence of the "profitability channel" and endogenous technical change.

In the models presented, a higher RER is favorable in the short run to capital accumulation and employment growth because it reduces the product wage in the traded goods sector with a positive effect on the sector's profitability. In the absence of technical progress, the gains in employment due to the higher rate of accumulation are reversed in the long run while the real wage returns to its initial value. With endogenous productivity change, the employment gains are not reversed and the steady-state value of the real wage increases as a result of the higher employment rate (which favors the diffusion of new technologies reducing labor costs) and the higher capital–labor ratio which, through embodied technical progress and technological externalities, raises the economy's productivity.

APPENDIX

This appendix presents a fuller analysis of the stability of the long-run equilibrium. For simplicity we leave aside technical progress. The analysis of long-run adjustments and the resulting equilibrium involves a system of two differential equations. The first, showing the dynamic behavior of the real wage, is derived from the wage inflation equation and can be expressed in reduced form in the following equation:

$$(W/P)\hat{} = F(L/N, W/P) \quad F_1 > 0,\ F_2 < 0 \qquad (3.A1)$$

The second equation, showing the dynamic behavior of the employment rate, has the following reduced form:

$$(L/N)\hat{} = G(L/N, W/P) \quad G_1 < 0,\ G_2? \qquad (3.A2)$$

The sign restrictions on the partial derivatives follow from the analysis in the text. They imply that the locus of real wage stability, $(W/P)\hat{} = 0$, is positively sloped, while the locus of employment stability, $(L/N)\hat{} = 0$, may be positively or negatively sloped depending on whether the effect of W/P on $(L/N)\hat{}$ is positive or negative. The effect of a higher W/P is to reduce wage inflation, which tends to increase the employment growth rate (making G_2 positive), but a higher W/P reduces u, the output-capital ratio (as exports and the volume of output fall), which has a negative effect on the rate of capital accumulation and the growth of employment (making G_2 negative). We have therefore to distinguish two cases: (1) $G_2 < 0$, yielding a negatively sloped $(L/N)\hat{} = 0$ locus; (2) $G_2 > 0$, yielding a positively sloped locus.

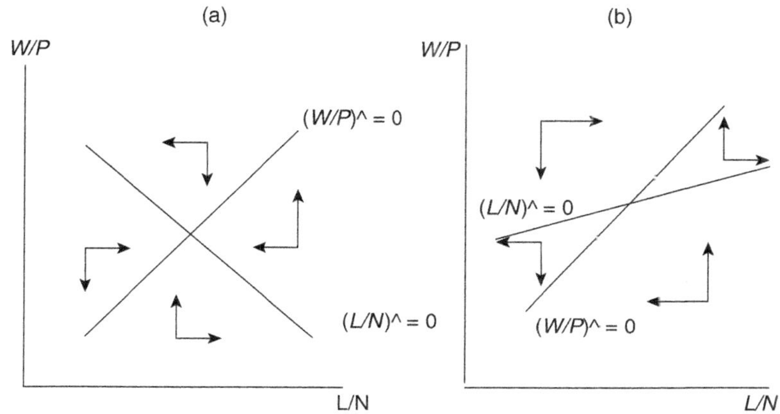

Figure 3.A.1 Long-run Dynamic Adjustments.

Case 1 is depicted in Figure 3.A.1(a), which reproduces Figure 3.2 in the text. It can be shown easily that given the sign restrictions of the partial derivatives, the system has a negative trace and positive determinant. The equilibrium is thus stable and the economy converges in the long run to the intersection between the two loci.

Case 2 may feature instability if G_2 is very large, that is, if the effect of a real wage fall on wage inflation is very strong. In this case, as shown in Figure 3.A.1(b), the slope of the $(L/N)^\wedge = 0$ locus is positive and less than the slope of the $(W/P)^\wedge = 0$ locus. The intersection is then a saddle point. The instability can be explained with the example of a devaluation starting from an initial long-run equilibrium. The resulting fall in the real wage triggers a rapid process of wage inflation, so rapid that the positive effect on employment growth resulting from the higher profitability is offset by the negative effect on employment growth arising from wage growth. The employment rate then falls, moving the economy away from the initial long-run equilibrium. By contrast, if G_2 is positive but relatively small so that the $(L/N)^\wedge = 0$ locus is steeper than the $(W/P)^\wedge = 0$ locus the economy converges to the long-run equilibrium with a warranted growth rate equal to the natural rate.

4

The Dutch Disease, the Staple Thesis, and the Recent Natural Resource Boom in South America*

This chapter addresses the subject of the adverse developmental effects of the Dutch disease: the theory, the experience of South America over the last decade, and the economic policy management issues concerning what to do about it. The chapter is organized as follows. The first section discusses the mechanisms (not confined to real exchange rate appreciation) through which a natural resource boom can lead to deindustrialization and also the conditions under which such a boom could have favorable developmental effects. I then turn in the second section to review the trends toward real appreciation and falling industrial profitability that have prevailed during most of the last decade in a number of South American economies. The third section discusses what can economic policy do to neutralize the adverse developmental effects of the Dutch disease. A final section concludes.

The Developmental Effects of the Dutch Disease: The Theory

Concern with the Dutch disease arises primarily from the real exchange rate effects of a natural resource boom (or of a surge in capital inflows) and the negative implications for long-term growth of the resulting contraction of industrial output, investment, and employment. These implications are negative to the extent that economic development is associated with the growth of modern tradable goods sectors operating under increasing returns to scale. The expansion of these activities generates endogenous productivity growth, within these sectors and elsewhere in the economy, due to the presence of internal economies of scale as well as positive external effects such as learning by doing externalities.

In order to formally illustrate the developmental effects of a natural resource boom, I will be using small open economy models with a natural resource intensive sector and a manufacturing industry. To begin with, consider a small open economy with two tradable good sectors, agriculture (A) and manufacturing (M). Both sectors use labor (L) and there are two specific factors: land (T) in agriculture and capital (K) in manufacturing. Agriculture operates under constant returns to scale and there are increasing returns to scale in manufacturing resulting from the presence of technological externalities (such as learning by doing externalities) associated to the size of the capital stock. The production functions are:

$$A = B\, T^b\, L_A^{1-b} \quad M = (K\sim)^{\mu}\, K^a\, L_M^{1-a}$$

where $(K\sim)^{\mu}$ is the external effect of the average capital stock.[1] Both goods are consumed and, in addition, good M can be invested. Labor is intersectorally mobile.

Along with sectors A and M, a sector S produces nontradable consumer services by means of labor under constant returns and using one unit of labor to produce one unit of output:

$$S = L_S \tag{4.1}$$

A fraction (q) of the rents (R) generated in sector A is spent on nontradables (I ignore, for simplicity, consumption of services by sector M):

$$p_S\, S = q\, R = q\, R\,(w,\, T,\, p_A)\;\; R_1 < 0,\, R_2,\, R_3 > 0 \qquad (4.2)$$

where p_S is the price of non-tradables in terms of good M. With a uniform wage rate, and given production conditions in sector S, this price is the same as the manufacturing product wage (w). Substituting from (4.1) into (4.2) and solving for L_S:

$$L_S = (q/w)\; R\,(w,\, T,\, p_A) \qquad (4.3)$$

which shows the level of employment in the nontradable goods sector as an inverse function of the wage, and an increasing function of the land endowment and the relative price of agricultural goods (p_A). Workers who do not find employment in sectors A and M, self-employ themselves in sector S. There is therefore no open unemployment. Using (4.3) and the full employment condition ($L = L_A + L_M + L_S$), the schedule of labor market equilibrium is given by:

$$L = L_A\,(w,\, p_A,\, T) + L_M\,(w,\, K) + (q/w)\; R\,(w,\, T,\, p_A) \qquad (4.4)$$

As shown in the LL curve in Figure 4.1, this schedule of labor market equilibrium is upward sloping in (ln w, ln K) space, where ln refers to the natural logarithm. Indeed, a larger capital stock generates in equilibrium higher real wages through its effect on the demand for labor in manufacturing. The position of the curve depends on the natural resource endowment and relative prices. An increase in the relative price of agricultural goods or an increase in the supply of land, both shift the LL curve upward: given K, both of these factors increase the demand for labor in agriculture and services (through the higher demand for services resulting from the larger agricultural rents). Labor market equilibrium requires a reallocation of labor away from manufacturing and the wage in manufacturing must rise in order to make this possible. The result is as expected: a greater abundance of natural resources, *given* other factor endowments, makes the country more prosperous, if we

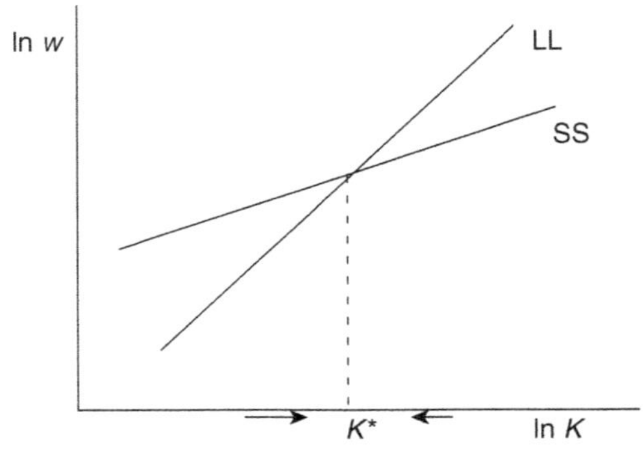

Figure 4.1 The Determination of Long Run Equilibrium Wages and Capital Stock.

take the real wage, as we shall in what follows, as a general indicator of living standards.

However, other factor endowments will not remain constant, at least not the capital endowment, which changes over time and in the long-run equilibrium will be determined endogenously. Assuming a stationary labor force and no exogenous technical progress, the steady-state condition in this economy simplifies to the equality between the rate of capital accumulation (I/K) and the depreciation rate of the capital stock (d): $I/K = d$. The rate of capital accumulation is assumed to be an increasing function of the profit rate in manufacturing, the only capital-using sector. The profit rate in turn is a function of the real product wage (inversely) and the level of productivity (positively), which increases with the capital stock given the presence of technological externalities. It follows then that, given the wage, the profit rate is an increasing function of the capital stock. The schedule of long-run equilibrium (the SS line in Figure 4.1) showing the value of the wage that satisfies the steady-state condition is therefore upward sloping: the higher is the capital stock, the higher is productivity and thus the real wage consistent with the equilibrium rate of accumulation (equal to the rate of depreciation).

At the intersection of the two schedules, the real wage and the capital stock reach their long-run equilibrium values. This long-run equilibrium is stable provided that the slope of the SS schedule is less than the slope of the LL schedule. This will be the case if returns to scale in the production of manufactures are not dramatically increasing (to the point of generating increasing returns to capital) (see Ros, 2013b). In these conditions, to the right of the equilibrium value of K (K^*) the market wage is higher than the wage required to generate a rate of capital accumulation equal to the depreciation rate. The capital stock then falls moving the economy back to the equilibrium value. The reverse occurs when the capital stock is below K^*: in this case the market wage is low and the profit rate generates a rate of capital accumulation higher than the depreciation rate.

Real Appreciation and Indirect De-industrialization

Consider the effects of a natural resource boom due to either a natural resource discovery or an increase in the relative price of natural resource intensive products. Suppose also that the higher rents arising from the natural resource boom are partly spent on nontradable goods and services (the spending effect in Corden, 1984) leading to a higher relative price of nontradables and thus to real currency appreciation. The higher wages and prices of nontradable inputs that manufacturing faces now cause a profitability squeeze in this sector that slows down capital accumulation and can lead to a new long-run equilibrium with a smaller manufacturing sector and larger natural resource and services sectors. The result is indirect deindustrialization (in the terminology of Corden, 1984; Corden and Neary, 1982) because, unlike direct deindustrialization to be discussed below, it results from real currency appreciation caused by the spending effect and depends on its strength. In the presence of increasing returns to scale in manufacturing, the new long-run equilibrium will not only feature a smaller manufacturing sector but also a lower real wage due to the adverse productivity effects of the contraction of manufacturing.

Let us follow the consequences of the natural resource boom in terms of the model above and with the help of Figure 4.2. As a result of a more abundant supply of land or a higher relative price of agricultural goods, the LL curve shifts upward due to a higher demand for labor in sector *A* and a higher demand for nontradables, which results from the spending of land rents. Note that this effect arises from the presence of nontradable goods, which implies that the LL schedule would shift upward even if the resource-intensive sector did not use labor directly. The spending out of higher rents leads to a higher relative price of nontradables and, thus, to a real exchange rate appreciation.[2] At the initial level of the capital stock in manufacturing, labor market equilibrium requires a reallocation of labor away from manufacturing and into services. If, in addition to being demanded by sector *A*, nontradables were used as inputs into manufacturing with a relatively inelastic demand, the adverse effects on manufacturing output and employment would, of course, be stronger. The economy moves from the initial long-run equilibrium at *A* to a new short-run equilibrium at *B* above point *A* with the same capital stock. This is not the end of the story, however. At point *B* the profit rate in

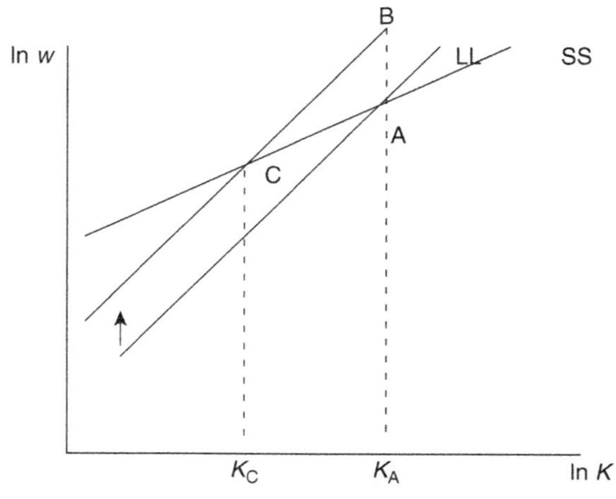

Figure 4.2 Deindustrialization Effects of a Natural Resource Boom.

manufacturing is lower than at point *A* due to the higher relative price of nontradables. The profitability squeeze in manufacturing slows down capital accumulation, which falls below the depreciation rate, and leads to a long-run equilibrium with a smaller manufacturing sector and larger natural resource and service sectors at point *C*. In Figure 4.2, the capital stock falls from K_A to K_C in the new long-run equilibrium. As a result of the adverse effects of deindustrialization on productivity, the real wage in the new long-run equilibrium is lower than initially (see Figure 4.2).

It is important to point out that the natural resource boom need not be permanent in order to cause adverse developmental effects. A real exchange rate appreciation resulting from a temporary resource boom can shift the pattern of specialization of an economy in an irreversible way and lock in the economy permanently as an exporter of primary goods. This is perhaps the main problem with natural resource booms. The fact that a transitory real exchange rate overvaluation that leads to a substantial decline in the investment and productivity of the nonresource intensive tradable goods sector (as productivity contracts endogenously with investment in the presence of increasing returns to scale), turns the sector unprofitable at the long-run equilibrium real exchange rate, thus causing a long-term, permanent contraction of the tradable activities other than the resource intensive sector.[3]

Capital Mobility and Direct Deindustrialization

In the presence of capital in the resource-intensive sector and capital mobility between the two tradable goods sectors, in either of the scenarios (higher primary product prices or new discoveries of natural resources), profitability in the natural resource sector rises at the initial level of the capital stock and above the level of profitability in the other tradable goods sectors (manufacturing, in particular). Capital moves then from manufacturing to the resource-intensive sector tending to equalize again the profit rates. The new equilibrium features a smaller capital stock in manufacturing and a lower real wage in labor market equilibrium, if manufacturing is more labor-intensive than the resource-intensive sector. The fall in real wages takes place even in the absence of increasing returns to scale in manufacturing (and thus in the absence of a decline in manufacturing productivity). The real wage contraction is caused by the fall in labor demand following the reallocation of capital away from the labor-intensive sector (manufacturing). With the given labor supply, the equilibrium wage falls then in order to clear the labor market. As Corden (1984) calls it, this is a direct deindustrialization effect because it is independent of what happens to the relative price of tradables in terms of nontradables (i.e., independent of real currency appreciation).

Let us follow more formally the consequences of the natural resource boom in a modified version of the small open economy model described above. We leave aside nontradables (to make clear that the spending effect plays no role in direct deindustrialization and the resulting fall in the real wage) and modify the production side of the model to allow for the use of capital in the resource-intensive sector (and neglect, for simplicity, labor input in this sector). This sector is thus an extractive industry (E) using capital and land (mineral land, specific to this sector) with a Cobb–Douglas technology: $E = K_E^b T^{1-b}$. Manufacturing is identical to the earlier definition, except for the assumption that it operates under constant returns to scale. This assumption will highlight that the mechanisms involved in the contraction of manufacturing and the reduction of real wages are, in this case, independent of the presence of increasing returns. Technology in sector M is thus described by: $M = K_M^a L^{1-a}$.

There are thus two specific factors: land in sector E and labor in sector M, with both sectors now using capital. With no intersectoral capital mobility, profit rates in these two sectors would generally be different since they include quasi-rents associated with the given capital stocks. Given the production functions in the two sectors, the short-run profit rates would be such that:

$$r_E K_E = [b/(1-b)]\ q\ T \quad (4.5)$$

$$r_M K_M = [a/(1-a)]\ w\ L \quad (4.6)$$

The wage rate (w) and rent per unit of land (q) are determined by equilibrium in the labor and land markets. Hence, we have:

$$T = T^d = K_E\ [(1-b)\ p_E/q]^{1/b} \quad (4.7)$$

$$L = L^d = K_M\ [(1-a)/w]^{1/a} \quad (4.8)$$

With capital mobility, quasi-rents will tend to disappear and profit rates become equalized. In equilibrium, the amount of capital invested in sector E must yield a profit rate equal to that obtained in sector M. The common profit rate (r), and the associated composition of the capital stock, must then satisfy:

$$K = K_E + K_M \quad (4.9)$$

$$K_E = (b\ p_E/r)^{1-b}\ T \quad (4.10)$$

$$r = r_M\ (w)\ r'_M < 0 \quad (4.11)$$

where (4.10), obtained by eliminating q from (4.5) and (4.7), expresses the relationship between the capital stock and the profit rate in sector E, and (4.11) shows the profit rate in manufacturing as an inverse function of the product wage.

Substituting (4.11) into (4.10) and using (4.9) yields the equation of a schedule of capital market equilibrium in (w, K_M) space:

$$K_M = K - [b\ p_E/r_M\ (w)]^{1-b}\ T \quad (4.12)$$

The wage rate and the capital stock invested in manufacturing are inversely related along this schedule (see the $r_M = r_E$

schedule in Figure 4.3). Indeed, a higher wage rate implies a lower profit rate in manufacturing (the labor-using sector). Restoring the equality between the two profit rates requires then a reallocation of capital toward the resource-intensive sector (which reduces the profit rate there).

To determine the wage rate and K_M simultaneously, we need to bring in the locus of labor market equilibrium. This is given by equation (4.8), showing the usual positive relationship between the wage and the capital stock (see the LL schedule in Figure 4.3): a higher capital stock in sector *M*, the labor-intensive sector, creates excess demand in the labor market thus raising the market clearing wage.

Consider the effects of a resource boom starting from an initial equilibrium at point *A* in Figure 4.3. The resource boom is caused by an increase in *T* or in p_E. In either of these cases, profitability in sector *E* rises at the initial level of the capital stock (K_E). In terms of Figure 4.3, the result is a downward shift in the capital market equilibrium locus: for each level of the wage, capital moves from the *M* to the *E* sector. The new equilibrium at *B* thus features a smaller capital stock in manufacturing and a lower wage. Corden (1984) labels this resource movement

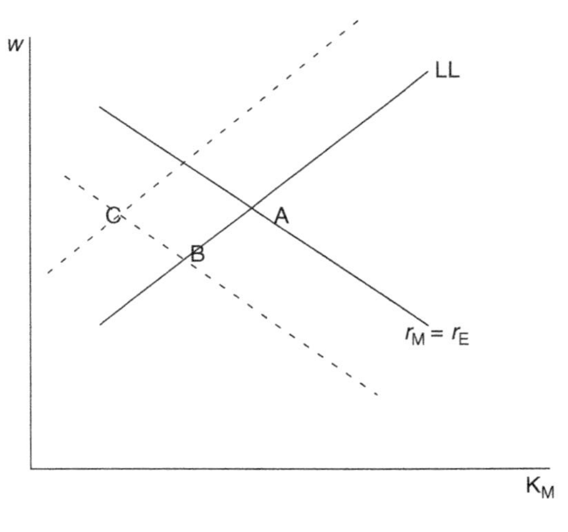

Figure 4.3 The Dutch Disease with Intersectoral Capital Mobility.

direct de-industrialization, because it is independent of the real exchange rate appreciation. Indeed, without nontradable goods, there is no spending effect and no change in the price of tradable relative to nontradable goods.

The reduction in real wages from *A* to *B* is not the result of a fall in manufacturing productivity under increasing returns to scale. The contraction is due to the fact that the higher profitability of sector *E* causes labor demand to fall following the reallocation of capital away from the labor-intensive sector. With the given labor supply, the equilibrium wage falls in order to clear the labor market.

It is easy to see that, in the presence of nontradable goods, a second resource movement will take place that counteracts the fall in labor demand but exacerbates the contraction of manufacturing. The spending effect will increase the relative price of nontradables and wages, causing profitability to fall in manufacturing. Capital then moves from manufacturing to the resource-intensive sector. This is *indirect deindustrialization* (see Corden, 1984; Corden and Neary, 1982). Unlike direct deindustrialization, it results from the real appreciation of the exchange rate caused by the spending effect and depends on its strength. In terms of Figure 4.3, it arises from the upward shift in the schedule of labor market equilibrium that leads to a new equilibrium at *C*, which features a higher real wage than at *B* but a capital stock in manufacturing that is even lower than at point *B*.

Latin America's Early Import Substitution Industrialization

An interesting implication of these models is that a fall in exports of primary products may accelerate industrialization. The fall in the profitability of the primary export sector and the resulting contraction in the demand for nontradables will cause resource movements and a real depreciation that can stimulate capital accumulation in manufacturing. Since, in the model, manufacturing is the importables sector, its expansion will appear as a spontaneous process of import substitution. Economists and historians in Latin America have noted these mechanisms in operation during the 1930s. At that time, the collapse of primary product export prices and volumes led to sharp real depreciations, which, often coupled with protective tariffs, triggered the beginning of the so-called early phase of import substitution in light manufacturing in a number of Latin American countries.

It was this process of spontaneous import substitution that Prebisch observed in the 1930s and recommended to accelerate, through protectionist measures, in the postwar period. Paradoxically, at first sight, Prebisch should have welcomed the lower terms of trade for primary commodities, as this trend was beneficial rather than harmful to industrialization in the periphery. Upon reflection, Prebisch is quite consistent: he saw as harmful the fall in the terms of trade that was *caused* by the expansion of the supply of primary products (as noted by Bhagwati, 1985). In the face of inelastic demands for primary goods, this expansion led to a skewed distribution of the gains from trade that favored the industrial centers of the world economy. This conclusion is quite consistent with the view that a reduction in world demand for primary products could and would change the pattern of specialization of the periphery in favor of manufacturing activities. This is what, in a less traumatic way, a protective tariff on manufactures can achieve: by changing the (domestic) terms of trade against the resource-intensive sector, it induces an expansion of the manufacturing sector.

The Staple Thesis and the Favorable Developmental Effects of Resource Booms

It is also important to point out that a natural resource boom can also have positive developmental effects, including crowding in effects on industrialization. This is the staple thesis view, originating in the work of Canadian economic historians, which emphasizes the role of linkages generated by different primary export activities and the nature of returns to scale in the sectors that benefit directly from the expansion of primary exports. Suppose, for example, that instead of being labor-intensive consumer services, as assumed in the model of indirect deindustrialization, the nontradable goods sectors that benefit from the increase in the natural resource rents and its spending operate under increasing returns to scale—transport infrastructure, say, stimulated by the expansion of the agricultural frontier—and that at the same time, the labor supply is elastic, due to the presence of surplus labor in the economy or to workers migration, so that the spending effects of the natural resource boom have little effects on wages. Under these conditions, the relative price of nontradable inputs (transport costs in the example mentioned) used by manufacturing will tend to fall, rather than increase, with the expansion of the primary export sector. The natural resource boom leads then to real exchange rate depreciation as the relative price of nontradables, in terms of manufactures, falls as a result of productivity increases (coming from the presence of increasing returns to scale in the production of non tradable inputs) that are larger than the rise of real wages (held down by the elastic labor supply). The consequence is an increase in the profitability and the rate of accumulation of the manufacturing sector that has positive long-term developmental effects. The spending out of rents has now an anti-Dutch disease effect.

Note that what is going on is the fact that the growth of the natural resources sector generates pecuniary externalities for the manufacturing industry through the expansion of the infrastructure sector and the *depreciation* of the real exchange rate (in the sense of a fall in the price of nontradables relative to tradables). The key conditions for the existence of these pecuniary externalities are the presence of an elastic labor supply and of increasing returns to scale in the production of nontradable inputs (see, on the subject, Ros, 2000).

To make more formally the basic point, consider the following open economy model. In addition to the natural resource intensive sector, there are two tradable goods sectors (S and M) producing a labor-intensive good (sector S) and a capital-intensive good (sector M). In each sector, technology is described by:

$$S = L_S \quad M = K^a I^{1-a} \quad 0 < a < 1,$$

where I represents the input of a set of non tradable intermediate goods:

$$I = [\Sigma\,(1/n)\, I_i^s]^{1/s} \quad 0 < s < 1,$$

n being the number of intermediate goods, assumed to be given.[4] Production of these intermediate goods is subject to internal increasing returns:

$$I_i = L_i^{1+\mu} \quad \mu > 0 \tag{4.9}$$

where L_i is labor input. The I_i goods may represent a set of producer services (such as banking and insurance) and manufactured inputs, as in Rodriguez-Clare (1996), or a set of infrastructural goods (power, transport, communications, training facilities), as in Skott and Ros (1997).[5] The key difference between traditional and modern sectors is that while sector M has a "backward linkage" a la Hirschman with sector I, there are no linkages in the case of sector S.

Firms maximize profits taking input prices as parametrically given. Producers in sectors S and M also face given output prices. In sector M, the capital stock is predetermined in the short run and since producers in this sector are atomistic, a firm's future demand and supply conditions will be independent of its own short-run decisions. Hence, there are no intertemporal complications. As shown in Skott and Ros (1997), the demand function for I goods is given by: $I_M = (1-a)^{1/a}\,(p_I/p_M)^{-1/a}\,K$, where

p_I (= $n\ p_i$ under symmetry) is the (minimum) cost of a bundle of intermediate goods yielding $I = 1$.

The terms of trade between good M and good S are determined in the international markets and are thus independent of domestic demand conditions. The resource-intensive sector produces traded goods with the same technology as sector A in the model of indirect deindustrialization. A fraction (q) of the rents generated in this sector is spent on I goods. Demand for I goods thus has two components: I_M, the demand from sector M that depends on the capital stock and the relative price of intermediate goods, and I_A, the demand from sector A, that depends on agricultural rents and therefore on land endowment and the price of A goods:

$$I = I_M + I_A = (1-a)^{1/a}\,(p_I/p_M)^{-1/a}\,K + qR/p_I$$
$$\text{where: } R = R\,(w, T, p_A) \quad R_1 < 0,\ R_2,\ R_3 > 0$$

In sector I, producers operate under conditions of monopolistic competition and face downward sloping demand curves:

$$I^d_i = D\,p_i^{\,-\emptyset} \qquad \emptyset > 1,$$

where D is a position parameter and $\emptyset$ is the price elasticity of demand facing individual producers. This elasticity is a function of s, a, and n, and, for a large n, is given approximately by $1/(1-s)$.[6] Inequality $\emptyset > 1$ follows from the parameter restrictions $0 < a < 1$ and $0 < s < 1$.

With a single intermediate good ($n = 1$), the monopoly producer of this good would clearly face an intertemporal optimization problem: the current price p_I would affect the profitability of sector M, which in turn could influence capital accumulation in sector M and thereby future demand for the I-good. With multiple I-goods this intertemporal link is weakened and the decisions of an individual producer have only minor effects on the aggregate output of intermediate goods and profitability in manufacturing. To simplify, I assume that the number of nontradable inputs is large enough that intertemporal aspects can be ignored. From the conjectured demand function and the production function, the optimal pricing decision for the I_i-producer is a markup over marginal cost:

$$p_i = (1 + z)\ \omega$$

$$\text{where} \quad 1 + z = [\varnothing\ /(\varnothing - 1)] \quad \omega = w/(1 + \mu)\ I_i^{\mu/(1 + \mu)}$$

w is the wage rate, ω is the marginal cost of labor, and z is the mark-up over marginal cost. The price of *I* goods thus increases with the wage rate and is a decreasing function of the scale of the *I*-sector. The price–wage ratio in this sector is a decreasing function of the scale of the *I*-sector and the demand for *I* goods increases with the capital stock and rents. Consequently, given the wage and the price of *M* goods, as determined in international markets, the relative price of *I* goods (p_I/p_M) is a decreasing function of *K* and *R*:

$$p_I/p_M = p_I\ (K, R, w/p_M) \quad p_{I1}, p_{I2} < 0; \quad p_{I3} > 0$$

Given the production conditions assumed in sector *M* (a Cobb–Douglas technology with two factors, *I* and *K*), the rate of profit can be expressed as a function of only p_I/p_M and the parameters of the production function. Since the profit rate is a decreasing function of the relative price p_I/p_M, we can express it, using the equation for p_I/p_M, as:

$$r = r\ (K, R, w/p_M) \quad r_1, r_2 > 0 \quad r_3 < 0$$

As long as it exists, the labor-intensive *S* sector provides a perfectly elastic supply of labor at a wage (in terms of *M* goods) equal to the price of the *S* good ($w = p_S$). This flat segment of the labor market equilibrium schedule (LL) is the consequence of the fact that both *S* and *M* goods are traded at given international prices and that constant returns to labor prevail in sector *S*. The LL schedule of the model is thus a horizontal line for $L_S > 0$. When $L_S = 0$, the labor supply is no longer perfectly elastic and the LL slopes upward.

Consider now the SS schedule along which the rate of capital accumulation is equal to the depreciation rate and the capital stock is stationary. The profit rate in sector *M* is an inverse function of the wage (w/p_M) and increases with the capital stock. Indeed, an increase in *K* raises the demand for *I* goods and reduces marginal costs in the *I*-sector. The fall in the relative price (p_I/p_M) (for a given value of w/p_M) raises profits in the *M* sector. Thus, the required wage that is consistent with the steady-state rate of capital accumulation is an increasing function of the capital stock. The new feature now is that the profit rate in sector *M* also increases with a higher demand for *I* goods coming from a higher spending out of agricultural rents. The profit rate (and thus the required wage) being an increasing function of rents, the position of the SS schedule depends on the abundance of land (and on the fraction of rents, q, spent on *I* goods).

Multiple equilibria are a possibility. Figure 4.4 illustrates this case. Points *L* and *H* are stable equilibria: a small departure to the right of *L* or *H* makes the market equilibrium wage too high to generate the equilibrium rate of accumulation (equal to the depreciation rate), consistent with the wage on the SS schedule, while a small departure to the left of *H* makes the market wage less than required to generate the equilibrium rate of accumulation. The rate of accumulation is then higher than the depreciation rate and the capital stock expands. By implication the low *K* intersection at *U* is an unstable equilibrium: a small departure from it sets in forces that move the capital stock away from its value at the intersection.[7] The low level stable equilibrium at point *L* does not have an *M* sector. A small *I*-sector coexists with sectors *A* and *S*, but produces at such high costs that it is unprofitable to invest in sector *M*. In the high level stable equilibrium at *H*, there is no *S* sector: its labor force has been absorbed by a large sector of intermediate inputs producing at low costs for both the *M* and *A* sectors.

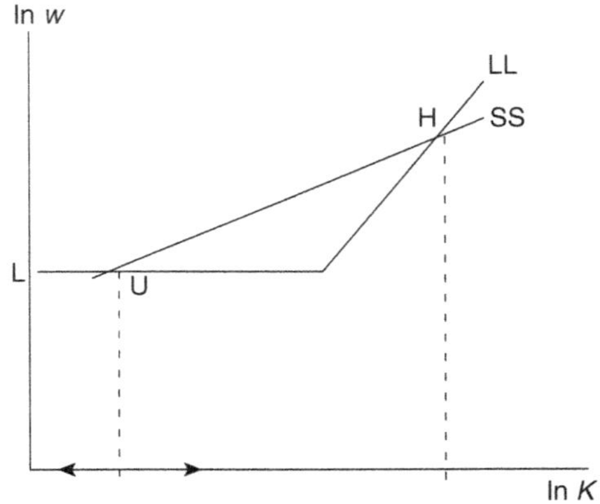

Figure 4.4 A "linkage effects" Model in an Open Economy.

The unstable equilibrium corresponding to the low *K* intersection at point *U* shows the size of the investments required to make the *M* sector viable.

Consider now the effects of a greater abundance of natural resources. The SS schedule shifts upward given that the higher rents spent on *I* goods reduce the relative price of intermediates and increase the value of the wage consistent with a given rate of capital accumulation. This has a number of effects. First, the greater abundance of land lowers the threshold value of the capital stock required to overcome a development trap, as the resulting expansion of the *I*-sector reduces production costs in the *M* sector. Second, for an economy with a capital stock larger than the threshold value but in the horizontal segment of the *w* curve, the induced reduction in the price of *I* goods increases the rates of profit and accumulation in sector *M*. The spending of agricultural rents has now an effect exactly opposite to a Dutch disease. This is so because the spending effect in this case is equivalent to a real depreciation since it leads to a reduction in the relative price of nontradable *I* goods (and thus to an increase in the relative price of tradable goods, in particular in the relative price p_M/p_I). Third, the real wage in the high level equilibrium tends to increase even though this may be partly or completely offset by the upward shift of the LL schedule in the segment in which it has a positive slope. This upward shift reflects the more traditional Dutch disease effect. Note that this upward shift of the LL schedule does not take place at low levels of the capital stock since, for these values, the labor supply is perfectly elastic.

In sum, in the presence of linkages with an infrastructure sector subject to increasing returns to scale, the expansion of a natural resource–intensive sector generates pecuniary externalities to the manufacturing industry and can thus promote industrialization. Note that the generation of these pecuniary externalities requires an elastic labor supply. In the model presented, this elastic labor supply arises from the presence of sector *S*. In other versions of the staple thesis, immigration of workers can play a more important role in generating the elastic labor supply.

THE RECENT ECONOMIC PERFORMANCE OF SOUTH AMERICA AND THE DUTCH DISEASE

The Raw Materials Export Boom of the Past Decade

The years 2000s, especially after 2003 and before the "Great Recession" of 2009, witnessed a resumption of growth in most of Latin America, led by a process of rapidly expanding exports and a medium-term improvement in the terms of trade of primary goods, developments that were only temporarily interrupted by the crisis of 2008–2009.[8] Table 4.1 shows the change in the terms of trade in 2000–2008 and the rates of growth of exports and GDP for the period 2000–2012 for a group of five South American economies, exporters of primary goods and natural resource intensive manufactures, and Mexico. Peru, a mineral exporter, leads the table with an astonishing 17% annual growth in export value and a GDP growth rate of nearly 6% while the rest of the South American economies show also high export growth, respectable GDP

Table 4.1 Terms of Trade, Exports and GDP Growth in Several Latin American Countries (Annual growth rates 2000–2012)

Country	Terms of trade 2008 (2000 = 100)	Export volume	Export value	GDP
Peru	136.7	6.1	16.9	5.7
Colombia	138.1	6.1	13.7	4.3
Chile	164.7	4.1	12.5	4.1
Argentina	133.2	4.8	9.8	4.0
Brazil	110.4	5.4	13.1	3.3
Mexico	105.8	3.1	6.9	2.2

Source: World Bank, World Development Indicators.

growth rates, and a favorable evolution of the terms of trade, especially in the case of Chile which recorded a sharp terms of trade improvement.

These processes are part of an acceleration of growth in the periphery of the world economy specializing in the production and export of primary goods that is closely associated to the emergence of China, a gigantic and extremely dynamic economy, as a new industrial center and formidable purchaser of agricultural products, minerals, copper, and other raw materials in the world economy. Indeed, China's share in the total exports of the main South American exporters of primary goods has been rising sharply since 2000 suggesting an important role for China's growth in the expansion of South America's exports. China overtook the United States as Brazil's major trade partner in 2009, it is the second largest trade partner of Argentina, Colombia, and Peru, and the largest purchaser of Argentina's agricultural products, and it is Chile's major trading partner in Asia. Meanwhile, and not surprisingly, Mexico, which is the only manufacturing exporter in Table 4.1 and for that reason a competitor rather than a supplier for China, records, among the countries included in the table, the lowest rates of export and GDP growth as well as the smallest improvement in the terms of trade (an improvement that is due exclusively to the still significant share of oil, about 15%, in Mexico's total exports).

Appreciating Real Exchange Rates and Falling Industrial Profitability

While the dynamism of the Chinese economy and of the world demand for raw materials have had so far favorable short-term effects on the economic growth of South American countries, the medium- and longer-term developmental consequences of the raw materials export boom depend on its effects on real exchange rates and the profitability of the nonresource-intensive tradable goods sectors, that is, on whether a Dutch disease is developing in the region. As shown in Figure 4.5, the raw materials export boom has been accompanied by a substantial appreciation of real exchange rates in Latin America sometime after the beginning of the past decade, only briefly interrupted by the temporary depreciations that took place in 2008 an early 2009 as a consequence of the international financial crisis, the "flight to quality", and the increase in risk spreads in emerging markets.

Figure 4.6 assesses the extent of appreciation by comparing the level of the real exchange rate in 2010 with its average level for the period 2002–2008 and the minimum level (i.e., the most appreciated level) in the 1990s. With the exception of Argentina, real exchange rates in 2010 were similar or lower

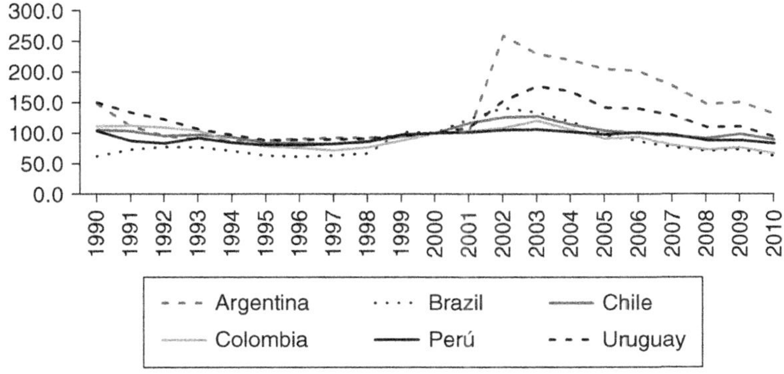

Figure 4.5 Real Exchange Rates in Several South American Countries.

Source: Frenkel and Rapetti (2011). Bilateral rates vis a vis the United States (2000 = 100).

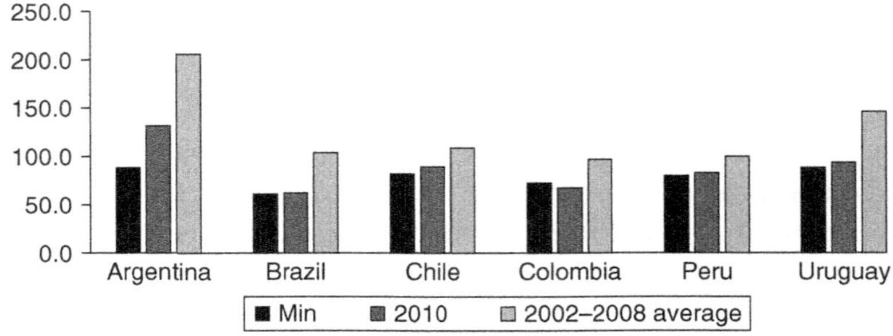

Figure 4.6 Real Exchange Rates in South American Countries. Minimum Level of the 1990s, Average of 2002–2008 and 2010.

Source: Frenkel and Rapetti (2011). Bilateral rates vis a vis the United States (100 = 2000).

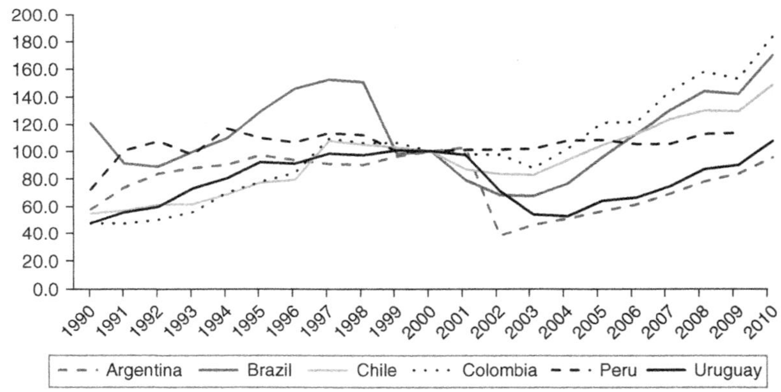

Figure 4.7 Unit Labor Costs in US Dollars in Several S. American Countries (2000 = 100).

Source: Frenkel and Rapetti (2011).

than the minimum levels of the 1990s and well below (including Argentina) the average levels of 2002–2008. The expansion of the natural resource–intensive sectors is clearly not having an anti-Dutch disease effect along staple thesis lines. This is why the primary exports boom has led to a decline in the profitability of the industrial sector. As shown in Figure 4.7, in the great majority of the South American countries considered, unit labor costs in dollars tended to increase after 2002–2003

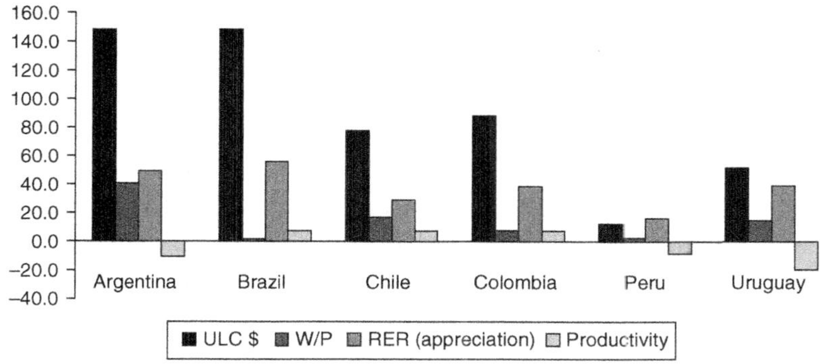

Figure 4.8 Increase in Unit Labor Costs in US Dollars and Its Determinants in Several South American Countries (Percentages).

in a substantial and sustained way suggesting that, at least for the labor-intensive tradable goods sectors, there is an important problem of competitiveness and profitability.[9]

Figure 4.8 shows for the same South American countries the results of a decomposition exercise, which measures the influence of the increase in the real wage, the real appreciation of the exchange rate, and the change in relative productivity on the increase in unit labor costs. What emerges clearly from the exercise is that the real appreciation of the exchange rate has had in all countries a major role in the increase in unit labor costs and, thus, in the decline in industrial profitability.

What Can Economic Policy Do?

How to counteract the adverse developmental effects of the Dutch disease? Since these effects arise mostly, although by no means exclusively, from the real exchange appreciation that accompanies the expansion of primary exports and its crowding out effects on nonresource-based tradable sectors, exchange rate policy has a crucial role to play in neutralizing the Dutch disease. If this is so, the inflation-targeting regimes currently fashionable in Latin America are not well prepared for the task of addressing those adverse developmental consequences.[10]

In fact, under this regime there seems to be a built in bias toward the appreciation of the exchange rate. Figure 4.9 shows the evolution of real exchange rates in Latin America in three groups of countries according to monetary policy regime (inflation targeting cum floating exchange rates, dollarized regimes, and others). As shown in the figure, the trend toward real appreciation in the period 2002–2013 (especially up to 2008 before the "flight to quality") was much more marked in countries with inflation targeting regimes than in the other two groups of countries.

This built-in bias toward appreciation may be due to various factors. First, under inflation targeting (especially in its "strict form," which involves the central bank reacting only to changes in the price level) monetary policy focuses on achieving low inflation using the interest rate as the main policy instrument while ignoring other policy objectives such as employment and growth. Given the relatively large impact of the nominal exchange rate on the price level—relative to that of the interest rate operating on interest sensitive components of aggregate demand, as argued below—it becomes in these conditions very

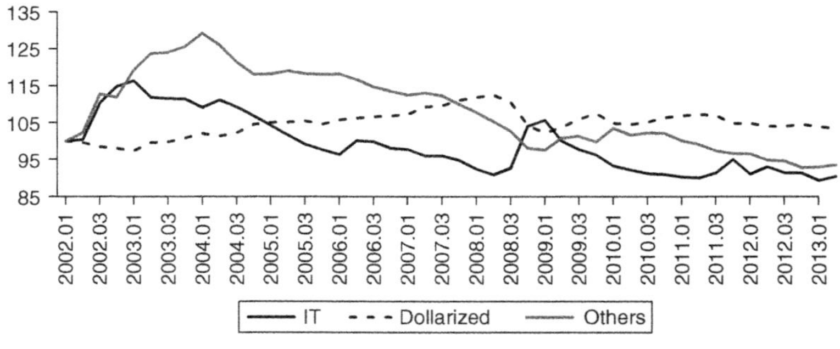

Figure 4.9 Real Exchange Rates in Latin American Countries According to Their Monetary Policy Regime, 1Q2002–2Q2013 (index 100 = first quarter of 2002).

Note: The group of IT countries consists of Brazil, Chile, Colombia, Mexico, and Peru. Dollarized countries include Ecuador, Panama and El Salvador. Others includes Bolivia, Costa Rica, Dominican Republic Honduras, Paraguay, Uruguay, and Venezuela.

Source: CEPALSTAT.

tempting for central banks to subordinate the exchange rate to their inflation objectives or to respond in a nonsymmetrical way to appreciations and depreciations.[11] Second, due to the shallowness of credit markets in developing countries the sensitivity of aggregate demand to interest movements is low and therefore central banks may need to raise interest rates excessively to achieve the inflation target. High interest rates attract capital inflows (a form of Dutch disease), which tend to appreciate the domestic currency.

Freeing monetary policy from the straight jacket of inflation targeting is thus a precondition for targeting the exchange rate. This may require the use of sterilized interventions in the foreign exchange market and the adoption of capital account regulations. However, these policies face limitations—as sterilization may run into significant quasi-fiscal costs and capital inflows may find ways to circumvent regulations—and financial integration implies that when exchange rate policy is trying to pursue a real exchange rate target, monetary policy is no longer completely autonomous. In addition, while exchange rate management can affect closely the absolute price of tradable goods it faces more difficulties when it comes to affect the relative price of tradables vis-a-vis nontradables and labor. If instead of generating a real depreciation, nominal devaluations lead to rises in domestic prices, the devaluation–inflation spiral resulting from engaging in further devaluations can have deleterious effects on capital accumulation and growth.

All this means that the job of counteracting the Dutch disease requires not only giving monetary policy a greater room for maneuver in order to target the exchange rate but also policy coordination through the help in particular of fiscal policy and wage management policies (see Frenkel and Rapetti, 2011, 2012; Rapetti, 2011). Indeed, fiscal policy may have to play a more preponderant role in managing domestic aggregate demand and in restraining, in particular, inflationary pressures in the nontradable goods sectors (see, on the subject, Eichengreen, 2007; Frenkel, 2008; Rapetti, 2011). Since part of the real appreciation associated to the Dutch disease arises from the spending out of natural resource rents on nontradable goods and services, counteracting this may require an increase in the fiscal surplus in order to moderate the pace of nontradable demand growth. The required increase in the fiscal surplus can be partly generated through tariffs or taxes on the primary exports which are at the origin of the Dutch disease (see, on the subject, Bresser-Pereira, 2008, 2011).

Wage management policies that coordinate the pace of real wage increases with the rate of productivity growth in the tradable goods sector can also help in restraining inflationary pressures in nontradable goods prices and in containing the growth of unit labor costs, thus preventing the fall in profitability and capital accumulation in nonresource-intensive tradable goods sectors. As argued in chapter 3, while a higher real exchange rate implies that in the short-run real wages are lower than otherwise, it will nevertheless lead to higher real consumption wages in long-run equilibrium as a result of the endogenous productivity growth effects of capital accumulation in the tradable goods sectors and of the absorption of employment from low-productivity nontradable goods sectors (which raises productivity there). The mechanisms connecting an initially higher real exchange rate and a higher value of the real wage in the steady state are the presence of increasing returns to scale in the tradable goods sector and of diminishing returns to labor in the nontradable goods activities.

CONCLUSIONS

This chapter has examined the mechanisms through which natural resource booms, triggered by either high raw material prices in international markets or the discovery and exploitation of newly discovered resources, can have negative or positive developmental effects in the long run. It has also argued that judging from the processes of real appreciation and declining industrial profitability and competitiveness that have characterized the South American economies benefiting from the booming world demand for raw materials in most of the past decade, a Dutch disease with negative long-run developmental effects has developed in the region. These effects have been reinforced by large short-term capital inflows. The slowing down of growth in several South American countries since 2012 may be an initial sign of these adverse developmental effects. Finally, I have argued that to counteract the negative long-run effects of the Dutch disease, a reform of monetary and fiscal policies is necessary together with a close macroeconomic coordination of these policies with wage management strategies.

5

Close to the Epicenter: Mexico and Canada during the Great Recession*

Canada and Mexico, the two minor partners of the North American Free Trade Agreement (NAFTA), have very different levels of economic development. In spite of this, their economies have a number of common features. First, both economies have traditionally had a privileged link with the United States in foreign trade (that manifests itself in the enormous weight of the United States in exports and imports of the two countries). Second, as a consequence of NAFTA they have tended to converge in their degrees of openness (currently in the two countries foreign trade accounts for around two-thirds of GDP). Third, they have similar export structures dominated by industrial products and a significant share of oil.

This chapter examines the comparative economic performance of Canada and Mexico since they came, with the United States, to be part of NAFTA in 1994. The analysis pays special attention to the behavior of the two economies during the international crisis and recession of 2008–2009 that had particularly severe effects in both cases because the United States, its main trading partner, was the epicenter of the crisis. The chapter's first section examines the main trends of their macroeconomic and trade performance under NAFTA. The second section briefly compares the two economies on the eve of the 2008–2009 crisis, 14 years after the beginning of NAFTA, in order to motivate the question of why the recession of 2009 was more severe in Mexico than in Canada. The third section discusses the evolution of GDP, as a whole and by major sectors of economic activity, and that of the components of aggregate demand during the crisis and recession of 2008–2009 and the subsequent recovery from the third quarter of 2009 to the third quarter of 2011. The fourth section assesses the economic impact of the US recession on the exports of the two countries and the role of other channels of transmission such as the capital account and, in the case of Mexico, migration and family remittances. The fifth section presents an analysis of the role that fiscal, monetary, and exchange rate policies had in mitigating or deepening the impact of the external shock of 2008–2009. A final section summarizes the main findings and conclusions.

MACROECONOMIC AND TRADE PERFORMANCE SINCE THE BEGINNING OF NAFTA

Basic Indicators of Macroeconomic Development

The analysis considers three periods: (1) the decade preceding the outbreak of the Latin American debt crisis in 1982 (1970–1981); (2) the so-called lost decade in the case of Mexico, which followed the debt crisis and lasted more or less until 1993 on the eve of the launching of NAFTA; and (3) the period since 1994 which NAFTA has been in force.

From 1970 to 1981, both countries recorded rapid economic growth (see Table 5.1), low unemployment, moderate growth in real wages (at a rate of 1% per year) and inflation on the rise, particularly in the case of Mexico. This decade was followed by a severe deterioration of the economic performance of Mexico (the lost decade) in which the GDP growth rate fell from 7% to about 1% per annum (1982–1993) and real wages declined at a rate of almost 1% per year, while inflation accelerated and reached an average rate of the order of 60% per year. Canada also

Table 5.1 Macroeconomic Development Indicators, 1970–2010

		1971–1981	1982–1993	1994–2010
Annual GDP growth rate (%)	Canada	4.0	2.1	2.7
	Mexico	6.9	1.3	2.2
Annual average inflation rate (%)	Canada	8.0	5.3	1.8
	Mexico	18.8	59.0	11.0
Real wage (Index 1993 = 100 and annual average growth rate, AAGR)	Canada	93.38	97.06	113.51
	Canada (AAGR)	1.23	0.36	1.52
	Mexico	106.77	84.75	92.50
	Mexico (AAGR)	0.94	-0.94	-0.17
Unemployment rate (%)	Canada	6.9	10.0	7.8
	Mexico	6.4	4.0	4.2
Real Exchange rate (Index 2005 = 100)	Canada	88.2	94.1	109.9
	Mexico	99.3	131.9	106.0

Note: The annual growth rate of GDP and the average annual growth rate of real wages refer to the periods 1970–1981, 1981–1993, and 1993–2010.

Sources:

GDP: Canada: Based on data from the World Bank, World Development Indicators (GDP at constant 2000 prices in national currency); Mexico: Based on data from INEGI (the average growth rate for Mexico is estimated with the GDP at constant prices of 1980 for the period 1970–1992 and GDP at constant 2003 prices in the period 1993–2010.

Inflation: growth rate of consumer prices, December-December. Canada: World Bank, World Development Indicators; Mexico: Banco de Mexico.

Real wage: Canada: index of real compensation of the private sector 1993 =100, OECD, Economic Outlook No. 88, December 2010; Mexico: index of wages, salaries, and benefits of the manufacturing sector 1993 = 100 (data available until 2008), published by Banco de Mexico (series of wages, salaries and nominal benefits deflated by the CPI).

Unemployment rate: Canada: total national unemployment rate (urban and rural unemployment), OECD, Economic Outlook No. 88, December 2010; Mexico: urban unemployment rate (data available since 1973), INEGI.

Real exchange rate: Estimated by the OECD on the basis of consumption relative prices. For both countries: OECD Economic Outlook No. 88, December 2010. A rise means depreciation.

recorded a lower GDP growth in this decade but was successful in reducing inflation and maintaining positive growth in real wages (although more moderate than in the previous decade).

Since the beginning of NAFTA, GDP growth recorded a slight improvement in both countries compared to the

1982–1993 period but remained below that of 1970–1981. There has been a successful stabilization of inflation at low levels in both cases, in the case of Mexico starting from very high inflation rates. Real wages have grown in Canada after 1994 at rates slightly higher than the historic ones while in Mexico they have decreased, as a result of a fall, initially very large during the crisis of 1994–1995, which was followed by a slow but sustained recovery (except in the case of the real minimum wage, which has remained stagnant; see Figure 5.1). These trends have been accompanied by a tendency toward depreciation of the real exchange rate in Canada and real appreciation in Mexico (if we compare the averages for the periods 1994–2010 and 1982–1993).

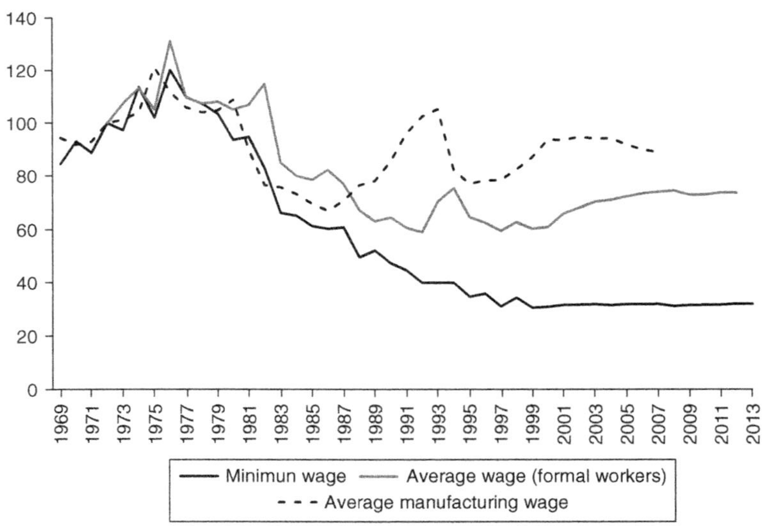

Figure 5.1 Mexico: Minimum Real Wage, Average Real Wage in Manufacturing and Average Real Wages of Workers with Social Protection, 1972–2010: (Index 1993 = 100).

Notes: (1) The manufacturing real wage includes wages, salaries and benefits in the manufacturing sector (data available only until 2008); (2) Average real wages of workers with social protection refers to those workers affiliated to the Mexican Institute of Social Security (IMSS).

Sources: Banco de México and IMSS.

Foreign Trade Performance

Two periods can be distinguished under NAFTA. During the first period, from 1994 to around 2000, the share of Canadian exports in total US imports remained stable at around 18–19% (see Figure 5.2) while that of Mexican exports, also as a percentage of United States imports, increased from less than 7% in 1993 to around 11% in 2000. In contrast, during the second period (2000–2010), the share of Canadian exports fell from 18–19% to around 14% while Mexican exports remained stable at 10–11% (in fact, there is a slight decline before 2009 followed by a recovery in 2009 and 2010).

To what extent is the slowdown in exports between 1994–2000 and 2000–2010 linked to the rise of China's exports after its entry to the World Trade Organization in 2001? Table 5.2 presents a decomposition exercise of the change in exports to

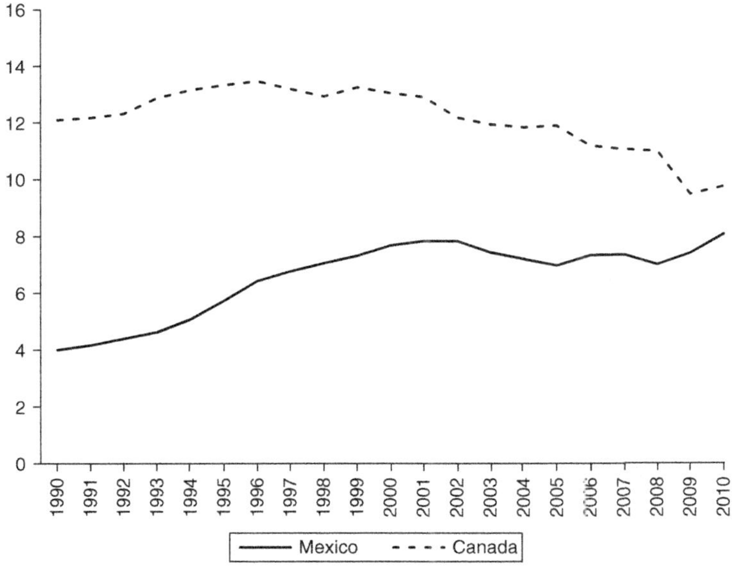

Figure 5.2 Canada and Mexico Share in United States Imports, 1990–2010 (% of total US imports).

Source: Based on Bureau of Economic Analysis of the US Department of Commerce.

Table 5.2 Components of the Change in US Exports [1993–2000 and 2000–2008 (percentage contributions)]

	Mexico	Canada	China
Demand effect			
1993–2000	49.0	98.2	41.9
2000–2008	105.4	158.6	21.1
Participation effect			
1993–2000	24.8	0.0	28.8
2000–2008	-1.3	-45.8	55.3
Interaction effect			
1993–2000	26.2	1.9	29.3
2000–2008	-4.2	-12.8	23.6

Note: The sum of the three effects is 100%.

Source: Based on data from ECLAC.

the United States by Mexico, Canada, and China during the two periods. This change can be attributed to: (1) the effect of demand, that is, the increase in the demand for imports by the United States (holding constant the initial share of each country in total imports); (2) the participation effect, that is, the increase in the share of each country in US imports (holding constant the total of these imports); (3) a residual attributable to the interaction between the demand effect and the participation effect. As can be seen from the table, in both Mexico and Canada there is a marked change of trend between the two periods in their participation in US imports: in the case of Mexico, it goes from a significant increase in 1993–2000 (that explains 25% of the increase in exports of Mexico to the United States, without taking into account the interaction effect) to a stagnation in 2000–2008, while in the case of Canada it goes from a stable participation in the first period to a sharp fall in the second. Accompanying these changes of trend is the evolution of China's exports to the United States. In this case the percentage of the change explained by the increase in participation rises significantly with the entry of China into the World Trade Organization in the early 2000s.

NAFTA Results and Initial Expectations

The expectations generated in the early and mid 1990s by the launching of NAFTA were great. The expected economic benefits of the process of integration of North America were considerable, especially for Mexico, one of the minor partners, and among the three partners, the one with lower economic development. General equilibrium models predicted at the time considerable welfare gains for Mexico arising from various types of gains from trade: the traditional gains from inter-industry trade (generated by the reallocation of resources according to the comparative advantages of the economy), those resulting from the expansion of intra-industry trade associated with increased exploitation of economies of scale, and those generated by the increase in foreign direct investment flows.[1] The expected benefits, of the order of 5% to 8.1% of Mexican GDP, were significant taking into account that NAFTA would not represent a radical change with respect to what had already happened since the mid-1980s as a result of Mexico's unilateral trade liberalization. In effect, the Mexican economy (not to mention the economies of Canada and the United States) was already, on the eve of NAFTA, very open to trade and capital flows (one of the most open among developing countries according to the Organisation for Economic Co-operation and Development [OECD]). Although less well-founded, the expectations based on the dynamic benefits of the integration, inspired by the experience so far of the European Community both in its initial stage and later when countries such as Spain, Ireland, and Portugal successfully integrated to it, anticipated a process of convergence through time in the levels of productivity, wages, and real income per capita within the new economic zone.

The initial expectations about the economic consequences of NAFTA were very far from being met. Indeed, as we have seen, Mexico's performance in terms of growth during the NAFTA period, although better than that of the lost decade, has been much poorer than in the 1970s (the annual growth rate of GDP was 2.2% in 1993–2010 compared with 6.9% in 1970–1981) and also poorer than that of the Canadian economy in 1993–2010. Real wages recorded on average a negative growth rate in 1993–2010 (see Table 5.1)[2] and have tended to diverge, rather than converge, with respect to the levels prevailing in the United States and Canada.

Although the expected benefits for the United States and Canada, with very open economies and an integration agreement between them before NAFTA, were much lower than for the Mexican economy, it is worth noting that if we judge from the fact that the Canadian economy grew during the NAFTA at a lower rate than in the period 1970–1981, these benefits may not have been met.

An Initial Comparison of the Two Economies on the Eve of the Recent Crisis

On the eve of the 2008–2009 crisis, around 15 years after the beginning of NAFTA, the economies of Canada and Mexico had several common features that were relevant to their performance during the crisis. On the positive side, banks and financial institutions in the two countries had much lower levels of exposure to high-risk credit markets than those that prevailed in the United States and other developed countries in Europe. This is particularly the case in Canada where the assets–capital ratio of major banks was on average of 18, compared with more than 25 in the United States, more than 30 for European banks and more than 40 for some of the large global banks. In addition, both Canada and Mexico had a relatively low public debt as a proportion of GDP. This, along with an initially solid fiscal situation (balanced budget in Mexico and a small fiscal surplus in Canada), gave them a considerable fiscal space to cope with the impact of the recession.

On the negative side, the two economies share a high degree of integration with the US economy, the epicenter of the international crisis. Both have a large degree of openness to foreign trade with high dependence on the US market and a significant participation in total exports of products such as oil or those of the automobile industry that were hit hard by the recession in the United States. In effect, as shown in Table 5.3, both countries have almost identical degrees of openness to foreign trade and concentration of their exports to the US market.

Table 5.3 A Comparison Between Canada and Mexico Around 2008

Concept	Canada	Mexico
Share of foreign trade in GDP (%)	67.8	66.9
US share in total in exports (%)	77	80
Correlation with US GDP cycle[1]	0.91	0.91
	(14.2)	(13.9)
Correlation with US industrial GDP cycle[1]	0.95	0.93
	(18.4)	(15.6)
GDP change in 2009 (%)	-2.5	-4.7

[1] The correlation coefficients refer to the period 2000–2011. *t*-statistics in parentheses.

Sources: Penn World Table 6.3 for degree of openness to foreign trade; Statistics Canada and INEGI for US share in exports; Statistics Canada and INEGI for GDP growth; Cuevas (2011) for the correlations between economic cycles.

Table 5.4 Goods Exports Structure, 2008 (percentages of total exports)

By Sector of Origin	Mexico	Canada
Products and electrical and electronic equipment	24.1	nd[1]
Automobile industry	19.1	12.5
Machinery and special equipment	9.6	18.9[2]
Other manufactures	26.5	31.7
Oil	14.9	12.5[3]
Others	5.8	24.4
By geographic area		
United States	80.2	75.7
Rest of America	10.0	nd
Europe	6.2	8.0
Asia	3.0	nd
Others	0.6	nd

[1] See third row (machinery and equipment).

[2] Machinery and equipment.

[3] The share of energy products is 25.7%.

Sources: INEGI, Mexico Historical Statistics, 2009; Bank of Mexico, Informe Anual, 2008, Statistics Canada.

In addition, the structure of exports is similar with a predominance of manufacturing exports and a significant share of oil in total exports (see Table 5.4). As a result of these characteristics, the correlation of the economic cycle of both economies with the cycle of total GDP and industrial GDP of the United States is very high (especially the synchronization of the industrial cycles) during the period 2000–2011 (see Table 5.3 and on this topic, Sosa [2008] and Cuevas [2011]).

Given these common features, it is remarkable how different were the performances of the two economies during the crisis, as reflected in the fact that the recession was much more severe in Mexico (a fall in GDP of 4.7% in 2009) than in Canada where the fall in GDP (2.5%) was one of the lowest in the OECD area (where the average decline was 3.5%). Another striking contrast refers, as we shall see in detail, to the speed of recovery in the aftermath, much faster in Mexico than in Canada to the point

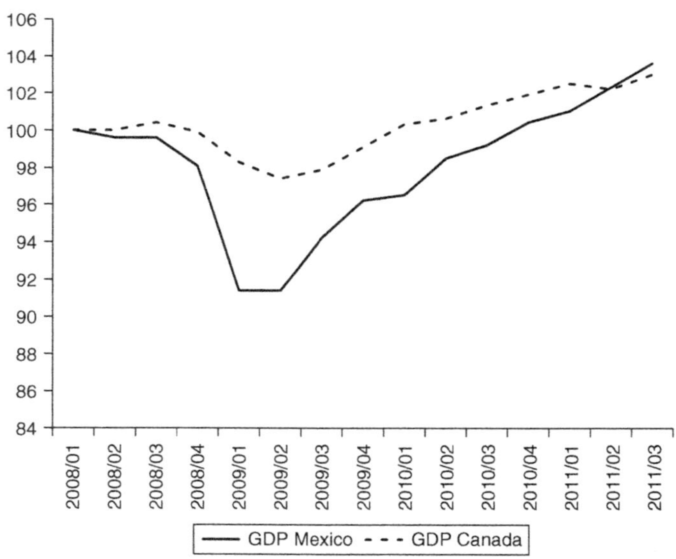

Figure 5.3 Canada and Mexico GDP: I-2008/III-2011 (Index I-2008 = 100).

Note: For Mexico, quarterly seasonally adjusted GDP at constant prices of 2003. For Canada, seasonally adjusted GDP at constant prices of 2002.

Source: Based on INEGI and Statistics Canada CANSIM.

that in the second quarter of 2011, the two economies were in a similar situation with a GDP that was about a percentage point below its level in the last quarter of 2007 (Figure 5.3).

Performance during the Crisis, Recession, and Recovery (2008–2011)

The international economic and financial crisis of 2008–2009 affected Canada and Mexico dramatically. The contraction in the level of economic activity and employment were substantial in 2008 and early 2009. In Canada, this meant the first recession of importance since the early 1990s. In Mexico, the drop in production in 2009 was higher than in 1983, triggered by the 1982 debt crisis, and not far in magnitude to that which occurred in 1995 during the Tequila crisis (the worst recession since the Great Depression of the 1930s). At the same time, the resulting employment contraction led to a sharp increase in the unemployment rate in both countries and, in the case of Mexico, also to a very significant increase in underemployment and poverty.

Output and Employment

Tables 5.5 and 5.6 show the evolution of GDP for the whole economy and by major sectors as well as some indicators of employment in Canada and Mexico. In Canada, the fall in manufacturing production starting in 2008-I accelerates in the fourth quarter of this year and ends up dragging the economy as a whole into a recession (Table 5.5). The sharp falls in the electricity and construction sectors also contribute to the recession. The recession deepens in the first half of 2009, driven by the industrial contraction (manufacturing and construction), while services, with a wide participation in the total, tend to be stabilizing by fluctuating less than the whole economy. Recovery begins in the third quarter of 2009, driven in part by manufacturing, so that the recession ended up being short. The unemployment rate increased 2.3 percentage points between

Table 5.5 Canada: Total GDP and By Sectors and Unemployment Rate. I-2008/III-2011 (Quarterly percentage variation)

GDP growth[1]	2008				2009				2009				2011		
	I	II	III	IV	I	II	III	IV	I	II	III	IV	I	II	III
Agriculture[2]	4.8	1.7	0.8	−0.2	-4.5	−3.9	−1.0	0.5	1.4	2.1	0.6	−1.0	0.4	1.0	−0.7
Mining	−0.2	−1.3	2.8	−0.5	-5.3	−5.8	−2.7	2.8	3.7	3.2	0.9	2.2	2.9	−1.9	3.2
Manufacturing	−3.2	0.2	−1.5	−4.6	-9.0	−3.2	1.5	1.7	3.5	2.6	0.5	−0.3	2.2	−1.1	0.9
Construction	2.0	0.7	0.3	-2.1	-6.7	-2.9	0.5	2.7	3.7	1.8	1.5	0.9	1.6	0.4	1.2
Electricity[3]	0.8	0.9	1.0	−1.5	-0.7	-2.3	-1.1	2.4	0.5	−1.1	1.6	0.7	2.9	1.3	0.7
Services	0.4	0.4	0.4	−0.3	-0.8	0.3	0.6	0.6	1.1	0.3	0.6	1.0	0.8	0.2	0.5
Total economy	0.1	0.3	0.2	−1.0	-2.5	−0.7	0.5	1.0	1.6	0.8	0.7	0.8	1.1	0.0	0.7
Unemployment[4]	6.3	6	6.2	6	8.3	8.4	8.5	7.8	8.7	8.0	8.2	7.2	8.1	7.5	7.4

[1] Percentage changes with respect to the previous quarter. The levels of total GDP and by sector are at constant prices of 2002 and seasonally adjusted. Total GDP and by sector are at basic prices.

[2] Includes forestry, fishing and hunting.

[3] Includes gas and water.

[4] Unemployment rate. Percentage of the economically active population.

Source: Based on Statistics Canada, *CANSIM*, and OCDEstats.

Table 5.6 Mexico: Total GDP and By Sectors and Employment Indicators. I-2008/III-2011 (Quarterly percentage variation)

GDP growth[1]	2008				2009				2010				2011		
	I	II	III	IV	I	II	III	IV	I	II	III	IV	I	II	III
Agriculture[2]	-0.7	3.3	-0.5	0.5	-2	-0.2	-1.6	-0.2	2.4	4.3	-1.9	1.0	-4.8	0.5	11.8
Mining	0.6	-2.1	0.5	0.7	-2.3	-0.9	0.1	-0.7	3.2	0.2	0.1	-2.0	-1.4	1.0	-1.3
Manufacturing	0.5	-0.1	-1.1	-2.6	-10.6	0.2	4.5	4.8	1.7	1.6	1.0	1.8	1.5	1.1	0.9
Construction	3.9	-3.6	0.5	-1.8	-3.8	-0.7	-1.2	-2	0.4	1.5	0.8	1.7	1.3	0.1	2.0
Electricity[3]	-1.3	-1.5	-2.3	1.1	1.8	0.4	1.3	0.8	-1.6	1.8	2.6	0.4	3.2	1.0	0.3
Services	0.8	0.2	-0.4	-0.5	-5.9	1.2	1.5	1.1	0.9	1.0	0.9	1.1	0.8	1.1	1.6
Total economy	0.7	-0.4	0	-1.5	-6.7	0	2.8	2	0.3	2	0.7	1.2	0.6	1.3	1.3
Employment indicators[4]															
Unemployment[5]	3.8	3.7	3.9	4.4	5.0	5.5	5.8	5.5	5.3	5.6	5.2	5.5	5.2	5.2	5.6
Underemployment[6]	6.6	6.8	6.7	7.4	7.9	10.8	8.7	9.3	9.3	8.6	8.4	8.1	8.1	8.2	8.9
Informal Employment[6]	27.4	27.5	27.1	27	28.2	28.1	28.2	28.3	28.6	28.8	28.0	27.2	28.5	28.9	28.7

[1] Percentage changes with respect to the previous quarter. Levels of GDP at 2003 prices and seasonally adjusted.

[2] Includes livestock, forestry, fishing and hunting.

[3] Includes water supply and gas by pipelines to the final consumer.

[4] Average rates of the quarter (seasonally adjusted data).

[5] Percentage of the economically active population.

[6] Percentage of the employed population. Underemployment refers to the employed population that would work more hours than the present job allows.

Source: Based on INEGI.

2008-IV and 2009-I, reaching its maximum value in the first quarter of 2010. By 2011-I it was still more than 2 percentage points above the level of 2008-IV.

In Mexico, the economic expansion after 2002 came to an end in the first quarter of 2008 and in the following two quarters the economy went into recession (see Table 5.6). Then, driven by the accelerating decline of manufacturing production, the overall level of economic activity contracted sharply in the fourth quarter of 2008 and the first quarter of 2009 (at a rate of –1.5% and –6.7%respectively). Construction was also severely affected by the economic downturn, while commerce and services fell reflecting the movement of total GDP. A change in the trend begins in the third quarter of 2009 and continues into the fourth quarter. In these two quarters total GDP grows at 2.8% and 2.0% with respect to the previous quarter. Just as in Canada, the recession turned out to be relatively short and driven by the contraction of industry, the manufacturing sector in particular. In contrast to Canada, however, the recession was very deep: in 2009-I, the worst quarter in the two cases, total GDP fell almost 7% in Mexico compared to 2.5% in Canada. This is so despite the fact that the contraction of manufacturing, the sector most affected in both cases, was similar (10.6% in Mexico and 9.0% in Canada, after a fall in the last quarter of 2008 that was greater in the case of Canada). We shall return later to comment on this contrast between the similarity in the behavior of the manufacturing industry and the difference in the depth of the recession in the economy as a whole.

The recession led to a significant deterioration of employment indicators. The unemployment rate increased by more than 2 percentage points between the second quarter of 2008 and the third quarter of 2009 (when it reached its maximum value of 5.8%) and started to fall only in the fourth quarter of 2009.[3] The underemployment rate recorded a similar evolution, increasing 4 percentage points and reaching a maximum value of 10.8% in the second quarter of 2009. This meant that the participation of the unemployed and partially employed in the labor force reached a level of around 15% in the second quarter of 2009. The share of informal employment in total employment also increased and continued to do so until the second quarter of 2011.

Aggregate Demand and Its Components

Tables 5.7 and 5.8 show the evolution of the main components of GDP in Canada and Mexico. In Canada, private investment (that had been stagnant since 2008-II) and exports were the components of aggregate demand that more sharply fell during the recession, declining during the fourth quarter of 2008 and the first quarter of 2009 at rates of –5.8% and –11.5% in the case of private investment and of –5.7% and –9.2% in the case of exports. However, beginning in the third quarter of 2009 both components of aggregate demand began to grow, thus promoting the recovery of the general level of economic activity. Government spending grew during the recession. The expansion was particularly strong in the case of public investment during the second half of 2009 (at rates above 6% in the last two quarters of the year), thus playing an important role in the economic recovery from the third quarter of 2009. In contrast to Mexico, where, as we shall see, the vigorous upturn in exports was the engine of recovery, in Canada export growth was rather slow and contributed little to the recovery. This contrast is explained, as we shall see later, by the different evolution of the real exchange rate against the US dollar in the two countries during the crisis and recession: while the Mexican peso depreciated sharply in the second half of 2008 and first half of 2009, the Canadian dollar showed a clear trend toward appreciation during 2009 after a moderate initial depreciation at the end of 2008.

In Mexico, exports were clearly the component of aggregate demand that fell more sharply during the recession, declining at rates of around 10% and 12% during the fourth quarter of 2008 and the first quarter of 2009 respectively, slightly more than in the case of Canada. From its highest point in the second

Table 5.7 Canada: Total GDP and Components of Aggregate Demand. I-2008/III-2011 (Quarterly percentage change)

Year	2008				2009				2009				2011		
	I	II	III	IV	I	II	III	IV	I	II	III	IV	I	II	III
Total GDP	–0.9	0.0	0.4	–0.5	–1.6	–0.9	0.5	1.2	1.2	0.3	0.7	0.6	0.6	–0.3	0.8
Private consumption	0.7	0.2	0.1	–0.6	–0.5	0.5	1.0	1.2	1.2	0.4	0.8	1.3	–0.1	0.6	0.2
Public consumption	1.5	1.3	0.4	1.0	1.1	0.4	1.3	1.3	–0.1	0.9	0.2	0.7	–0.3	0.3	0.3
Private investment	1.5	–0.3	0.1	–5.8	–11.5	–3.6	2.0	1.1	3.5	3.8	4.0	1.4	2.5	3.9	–0.4
Public inverstment	5.5	0.8	0.0	0.0	–0.2	2.5	7.3	6.2	3.0	3.7	3.9	2.1	0.3	0.9	–0.9
Exports	–3.3	0.5	–2.1	–5.7	–9.2	–3.8	3.2	2.4	1.9	3.5	–0.1	0.9	1.3	–0.9	2.8
Imports	–0.9	1.8	–2.4	–7.6	–11.7	–0.1	5.7	3.1	3.5	5.3	2.2	0.3	2.6	3.5	–0.9

Note: Seasonally adjusted series. Percentage changes with respect to the previous quarter. The total GDP and its components are at market prices of 2002.

Source: Based on Statistics Canada, *CANSIM*.

Table 5.8 Mexico: Total GDP and Components of Aggregate Demand. I-2008/III-2011 (Quarterly percentage change)

Year	2008				2009				2009				2011		
	I	II	III	IV	I	II	III	IV	I	II	III	IV	I	II	III
Total GDP	1.7	0.6	-1.5	-1.7	-6.6	-1.6	4.4	1.0	0.3	1.4	1.6	1.2	0.9	0.8	2.0
Private consumption	-1.6	1.1	0.2	1.4	2.9	-2.0	1.8	0.4	1.0	2.0	-0.9	-0.1	0.5	-2.0	2.1
Public consumption	-1.9	1.5	-2.0	-6.6	-7.7	-4.9	-0.7	-1.8	3.4	0.9	4.0	-0.5	10.4	2.1	-0.6
Private investment	10.9	2.8	10.4	5.1	-2.8	0.6	0.1	-2.0	3.2	1.6	-6.8	6.7	-22.0	12.7	7.8
Public investment	-1.4	2.5	0.3	-10.0	-12.0	-1.9	8.2	9.9	6.8	5.9	3.0	0.4	4.4	-0.3	-0.1
Exports	0.5	2.0	1.8	-12.0	-14.7	-4.9	10.9	7.0	7.6	4.3	2.9	1.2	1.5	1.1	2.2

Note: Seasonally adjusted series. Percentage changes with respect to the previous quarter. Levels of GDP at 2003 prices.

Source: Based on INEGI, Economic Information Bank (BIE).

quarter of 2008 to its lowest value in the second quarter of 2009 exports fell 21%. Private investment was also severely affected and it recovered late, unlike what happens with exports that started a vigorous recovery in the third quarter of 2009. In contrast to Canada where private investment begins to recover in the third quarter of 2009, in Mexico it did only in the first quarter of 2010.

Government spending as a whole tended to rise during the recession but much less than in Canada and contractions were recorded in public investment in the course of 2009 (and in public consumption in the second quarter of 2009). Unlike Canada, public spending (especially investment) does not appear to have played a significant role in the economic recovery from 2009-III. This role, as already mentioned, is played by exports in the case of Mexico.

The picture that emerges from the analysis is one of a predominantly industrial recession driven by the collapse of exports in both countries (to which one can add the contraction of private investment, especially in the case of Canada). Although the negative shock to exports was similar in the two countries, the fall in the overall level of economic activity was much more severe in Mexico than in Canada. The recession was followed by a relatively speedy recovery in which the expansion of public spending in Canada and exports in Mexico play the crucial role.

The Magnitude of the Shock to Exports and Other Transmission Channels

The Trade Channel and the Collapse of Exports

Among the several mechanisms through which the international economic crisis affected Canada and Mexico, the trade channel stands out to the extent that the United States, the epicenter of the global crisis, represents about 80% of the exports of both economies and foreign trade in these economies represent approximately two-thirds of GDP.

In both Canada and Mexico, the contraction of the value of total exports was largely a result of the fall of the price of oil and the volume of manufacturing exports. The value of manufacturing exports (around 95% of nonoil exports in Mexico and 90% in the case of Canada) fell 27% in Mexico and 20% in Canada in 2008-IV and 2009-I. Exports of the automobile industry, representing 26% of nonoil exports in Mexico and 22% in Canada, were particularly affected with contractions of 33% in Mexico and 28% in Canada during the first quarter of 2009. As a result, total exports fell 33% in Mexico and 30% in Canada in the fourth quarter of 2008 and the first quarter of 2009 (see Tables 5.9 and 5.10). Just as the exports contraction was slightly greater in the case of Mexico during the period of recession, in the phase of recovery starting in the second half of 2009 the dynamism of exports was also greater in Mexico.

The Capital Account Shock and the Fall in Private Investment

In addition to the initial deterioration of the current account, the balance of payments was affected by the "flight to quality," characteristic of situations of high uncertainty and increase in the demand for foreign assets. As can be seen in Table 5.11, in the case of Mexico, the capital account starts to deteriorate in the fourth quarter of 2008 and recorded a deficit of more than $6 billion in the first quarter of 2009, the product of a catastrophic collapse of portfolio investment flows (amounting to net outflows of almost $20 billion in 2009-I).

The flight to quality led to an increase of sovereign risk spreads on emerging market bonds, including Mexico, and a significant depreciation of the Mexican peso (which we will discuss in more detail below). The behavior of the capital account in Canada is the mirror image of what happened in Mexico (see Table 5.12). In this case the "flight to quality" meant capital inflows, rather than outflows, which makes the capital account, which had been in deficit in the first three quarters of 2008,

Table 5.9 Mexico—Exports of Goods: I-2008/III-2011 (thousands of millions of US dollars and percentage change)

Quarter	2008				2009				2010				2011		
	I	II	III	IV	I	II	III	IV	I	II	III	IV	I	II	II
Total	73.6	77.9	77.3	61.7	51.9	53.3	58	66.2	69.1	73.6	75.1	79.9	84.9	88.3	87.9
	2.8	5.8	-0.7	-20.2	-15.9	2.7	8.8	14.2	4.4	6.5	2.1	6.4	6.2	4.0	-0.5
Oil	13	15.4	14.6	7.3	5.6	7.3	8.3	9.6	9.7	9.9	10.1	12.1	13.4	14.8	13.7
	2.7	18.4	-5.3	-50.1	-23.3	29.8	14.3	14.9	1	2.4	2.2	19.5	10.8	10.4	-7.4
Non-oil	60.6	62.4	62.7	54.4	46.3	46	49.7	56.7	59.5	63.7	65	67.9	71.5	73.6	74.2
	2.8	3.1	0.5	-13.3	-14.9	-0.6	8	14	4.9	7.2	2	4.4	5.4	2.8	0.9
Manufactures	58.1	60	59.7	52.2	44.1	43.8	47.3	54.2	56.9	61	62.3	64.9	68.2	69.9	70.3
	2.8	3.2	-0.4	-12.6	-15.5	-0.8	8.2	14.5	4.9	7.3	2.2	4.1	5.1	2.5	0.5
Automobile	14.5	14.7	13.8	12.6	8.5	8.7	10.9	13.9	15.3	15.9	16.4	17.2	18.8	19.6	20.4
	2.2	1.5	-6.3	-8.2	-32.8	3.1	24.6	28.1	10	4	2.7	5.2	9.1	4.3	4.1
Other nonoil	2.4	2.5	3	2.2	2.2	2.3	2.3	2.5	2.6	2.7	2.7	3	3.3	3.7	3.9
	1.8	2.1	20.7	-25.9	-1.4	3.8	3.5	4.9	6	5.3	-2.1	10.7	11.8	8.3	7.6

Note: Series at current prices. The figures below the absolute values refer to the percentage change from the previous quarter.

Source: Based on INEGI.

Table 5.10 Canada: Exports of Goods–I-2008/III-2011 (thousands of millions of Canadian dollars and percentage change)

	2008				2009				2010				2011		
	I	II	III	IV	I	II	III	IV	I	II	III	IV	I	II	III
Total	106.3	118.7	120.3	110.1	85.2	80.2	82.3	86.9	89.8	94.7	91.2	98.6	99.6	102.4	106.3
	5.3	11.7	1.4	-8.5	-22.6	-5.8	2.5	5.6	3.3	5.5	-3.6	8.1	1.0	2.8	3.8
Oil	30.8	37.5	41.6	32.4	21.2	19.8	23.5	24.0	25.1	25.8	25.0	26.1	29.3	30.0	33.5
	19.5	22.0	10.9	-22.1	-34.4	-6.9	18.8	2.1	4.7	2.8	-2.9	4.3	12.4	2.3	11.5
Non-oil	75.5	81.2	78.7	77.7	63.9	60.5	58.8	62.9	64.7	68.9	66.2	72.5	70.2	72.4	72.9
		7.5	-3.1	-1.3	-17.7	-5.4	-2.8	7.0	2.8	6.5	-3.9	9.5	-3.1	3.0	0.7
Manufactures	68.3	72.7	70.7	68.8	56.7	52.3	52.3	55.9	58.2	61.8	59.2	64.1	63.2	64.1	64.6
		6.4	-2.8	-2.7	-17.6	-7.7	0.0	6.9	4.2	6.1	-4.2	8.2	-1.4	1.5	0.8
Automobile	16.8	16.7	14.6	15.6	11.2	10.9	12.2	14.5	14.0	15.9	14.2	15.2	15.0	14.5	14.2
	-10.4	-0.7	-12.5	6.6	-28.1	-2.3	11.1	18.8	-3.0	13.3	-10.3	6.6	-0.9	-3.9	-1.9
Other non-oil	7.2	8.5	8.0	8.9	7.3	8.2	6.5	7.0	6.4	7.1	7.0	8.4	7.1	8.3	8.2
		18.0	-5.7	11.1	-18.5	12.6	-20.7	7.7	-8.1	10.2	-1.6	21.2	-16.5	17.3	-0.7

Note: Series at current prices. The figures below the absolute values refer to the percentage change from the previous quarter.

Source: Based on Statistics Canada.

Table 5.11 Mexico: Balance of Payments I-2008/III-2011 (billions of US dollars)

	2008				2009				2010				2011		
	I	II	III	IV	I	II	III	IV	I	II	III	IV	I	II	III
Current account	-3.0	-2.2	-4.3	-6.8	-1.9	-0.2	-3.6	-0.6	0.4	-0.7	-1.8	-3.5	0.3	-3.0	-3.8
Financial account[1]	5.3	6.3	11.0	6.3	-6.1	-2.0	11.6	14.8	4.6	5.4	11.3	17.3	9.1	11.8	8.0
Foreign direct investment	7.7	6.5	5.3	5.8	1.9	4.8	1.0	1.2	2.6	0.9	-0.8	3.6	1.6	4.5	0.4
Foreign portfolio investment	-1.7	-3.6	8.2	7.5	-19.8	-1.9	6.5	9.9	8.8	4.2	15.9	0.2	9.5	9.2	13.9
Other investment	-0.7	3.4	-2.5	-7.1	11.8	-4.9	4.2	3.8	-6.8	0.3	-3.9	13.4	-2.0	-1.9	-6.3
Errors and omissions	1.6	-1.2	-1.8	-3.0	-1.6	-2.0	-1.7	-2.1	-3.2	-0.8	-1.3	-6.9	-1.8	-3.4	2.6
Change in net international reserves	3.9	2.9	4.8	-3.6	-9.7	-4.2	6.3	12.1	1.7	4.0	8.1	6.9	7.7	5.6	7.2

Note: This presentation of the balance of payments follows the criteria of classification and registration recommended by the International Monetary Fund in the fifth edition of its Balance of Payments Manual.

[1] Corresponds to the earlier concept of capital account.

Source: Based on data from Banco de México. Balance of Payments (2011).

Table 5.12 Canada: Balance of Payments I-2008/III-2011 (thousands of millions of dollars)

	2008				2009				2010				2011		
	I	II	III	IV	I	II	III	IV	I	II	III	IV	I	II	III
Current account	3.0	5.2	4.8	-7.7	-9.4	-10.4	-13.6	-11.8	-12.1	-12.9	-16.2	-9.6	-13.8	-14.9	-10.5
Capital account[1]	-2.7	-7.0	-5.6	8.4	8.3	9.9	0.6	14.9	8.4	13.0	15.3	10.2	11.2	14.2	9.4
Foreign direct investment (net)	-11.8	-5.6	-1.0	-3.8	-4.5	-4.7	-11.7	-2.4	14.3	-0.7	-10.2	-19.0	1.1	14.3	-9.3
Foreign portfolio investment (net)	7.0	27.1	-7.5	16.1	10.8	37.7	25.2	29.1	13.6	39.9	12.5	26.9	19.0	17.2	23.1
Others[2]	2.1	-28.6	2.8	-4.0	2.0	-23.1	-13.0	-11.8	-19.5	-26.2	13.0	2.3	-8.8	-17.2	-4.5
Change in reserves	0.2	-1.8	-0.8	0.6	-1.1	-0.5	-13.1	3.1	-3.7	0.1	-1.0	0.6	-2.6	-0.7	-1.2

[1] Change in reserves–current account. Includes statistical discrepancy.

[2] Capital account–FDI–foreign portfolio investment.

Source: Statistics Canada—Catalogue no. 67–001-X.

to be in surplus from the fourth quarter of 2008. In this (as in the opposite movement in Mexico) portfolio investment plays an important role. The net balance recorded strong surpluses between 2008-IV and 2010-II while foreign direct investment had a much more stable behavior (as in Mexico) and its net amount remained negative for almost all of the period.

The shock to the capital account was, therefore, in this case positive. This is also evident in the evolution of sovereign risk, which was very different from what happened in the case of Mexico. In Canada, the risk margin did not reach more than 160 basis points (compared with more than 600 basis points in the case of Mexico) and in February of 2009 had already fallen to less than 20 basis points. That is why the Canadian dollar, instead of recording a sharp depreciation as the Mexican peso did, reverses an initial depreciation rapidly throughout 2009 as we will see in more detail below.

It is worth noting the absence in both countries of a collapse of high-risk credit markets, as happened in the United States (as well as in other OECD countries like Ireland and Spain). Several factors prevented in both countries the development of a bubble in the housing market accompanied by a strong expansion of high-risk lending. In the case of Canada, this can be explained mainly by strong regulation of the banking system that has been a constant in the economic history of that country (see on the subject, Bordo et al., 2011). For different reasons—the low financial depth resulting from a downward trend in the ratio of bank credit to GDP—the Mexican financial system was not exposed to high-risk markets.[4]

THE ROLE OF FISCAL, MONETARY AND EXCHANGE RATE POLICIES DURING THE CRISIS AND RECOVERY

Fiscal Policy and the Size of the Fiscal Stimulus

The impact of the global recession on Mexico's public finances made itself felt through a fall in oil revenues (1.3 percentage points of GDP in 2009), partly due to a reduction in the domestic production of oil, and in tax revenues (0.5 percentage points of GDP; see Table 5.13).

How was it possible to maintain a small fiscal deficit (or even a balanced budget if we exclude PEMEX investments), in the midst of a moderate increase in public spending as a percentage of GDP and a sharp fall in the price of oil and tax revenues? There are several explanatory factors. First, the oil coverages implicated selling future oil at $70 per barrel in 2009 (double the level of late 2008) generating savings of around 118.4 billions of pesos (around $8.5 billion). Second, as we have already alluded to, in 2008 the balanced budget rule was amended so as to exclude the investments of PEMEX from the rule, a measure that reduced budgetary expenditures and generated an increase of 13% within the investment budget. Third, the depreciation of the peso tended to raise the domestic currency value of the oil export revenues. Finally, the government made use of non-recurrent revenues in the oil stabilization fund and in the operation surplus of the central bank for the fiscal year 2008 (SHCP, 2010a).

Table 5.13 Mexico: Public Sector Income and Expenditure, 2007–2010 (percentage of GDP)

	2007	2008	2009	2010
Total expenditure[1]	22.1	23.7	26.1	25.5
Primary expenditure	20.0	21.9	23.9	23.6
Financial cost of the debt[2]	2.1	1.9	2.2	2.0
Total incomes[1]	22.0	23.5	23.6	22.5
Oil	7.8	8.6	7.3	7.4
Nonoil	14.2	14.8	16.3	15.1
Tax income	9.3	9.9	9.4	10.0
Nontax income	1.4	1.2	3.2	1.4
Parastatal sector	3.5	3.7	3.6	3.8
Balance	0.1	-0.1	-2.3	-2.8

[1] http://www.apartados.hacienda.gob.mx/estadisticas_2001_2010/docs/2_ingresos/in01_015.pdf.

[2] Excludes compensated interest.

Source: Based on data from Ministry of Finance and Public Credit, 2011.

Table 5.14 Canada: Public Sector Income and Expenditure, 2007–2010 (percentage of GDP)

	2007	2008	2009
Total expenditure	37.8	38.4	41.3
Primary expenditure	34.8	35.6	38.4
Financial cost of the debt	3.0	2.9	2.9
Total income	39.5	40.4	41.4
Tax income	27.7	28.5	28.3
Non-tax income[1]	11.8	11.9	13.2
Balance	1.7	2.0	0.2

[1] Insurance premiums and health, contributions to social security, sales of goods and services, investment income, other income sources.

Source: Based on data from Statistics Canada.

The fiscal policy response was more aggressive in Canada. As shown in Table 5.14, public sector primary spending increased by nearly 3 percentage points of GDP in 2009, which led to an equivalent reduction in the fiscal surplus. The package of fiscal stimuli consisted of special federal funds for investments in infrastructure designed in collaboration with the provinces (OECD, 2011).

A comparison between the fiscal policy adopted by the two countries suggests, first, that the size of the fiscal stimulus was much smaller in Mexico than in Canada and, in fact, one of the smallest among OECD countries while that of Canada was one of the largest.[5] This should be assessed while keeping in mind that the size of the external demand shock was, in both cases, very high in the OECD context. Second, we must consider that the fiscal space for a bigger stimulation was available in Mexico. The central government debt as a percentage of GDP in Mexico was in 2007 the order of 25%, a very low value compared to other OECD countries. Comparing with Canada, it should be noted that the financial cost of the public debt in Mexico is less than one third that of Canada (Tables 5.13 and 5.14). More generally, in a group of 20 OECD countries only three (Australia, New Zealand, and Norway) had a debt ratio below that of Mexico that in turn had a debt as a percentage of GDP lower than, for example, the United States, Germany, United Kingdom, or France (OECD, 2009b).[6] The balanced budget rule in the fiscal responsibility act of 2006 prevented a greater mobilization of the fiscal space, as it probably did also the fear that a larger fiscal deficit would be accompanied by a deterioration in the rating of Mexican debt. The above comparison suggests that, given that the size of the external shock was slightly higher in Mexico than in Canada, the fiscal policy response could have been more aggressive in the case of Mexico.

Monetary Policy

In developed countries, the easing of monetary policy generally began before the third quarter of 2008. This is the case in Canada where the central bank, in the framework of an inflation-targeting regime similar to that of Mexico, reduced the target interest rate by 175 basis points in the first two quarters of 2008. In contrast, monetary policy in Mexico became more restrictive at the beginning of the crisis in response to the upward pressures on raw materials prices, the impact on the capital account and the resulting pressure on the exchange rate. The reference interest rate of the Bank of Mexico increased by 25 basis points in June of 2008 and again in July and August, and remained at 8.25% until January 2009. From then on, as the pressures on prices eased and the recession deepened, the interest rate was reduced in a series of actions by the central bank starting in January of 2009 (50 basis points) and continuing in February (25 basis points), March (75 points), April (75 points), May (75 points), June (50 points), and July (25 points), remaining from there constant at 4.50%[7]

Exchange Rate Policy

In the case of Mexico, after a gradual appreciation of the exchange rate in the first half of 2008 that took it to 10 pesos per US

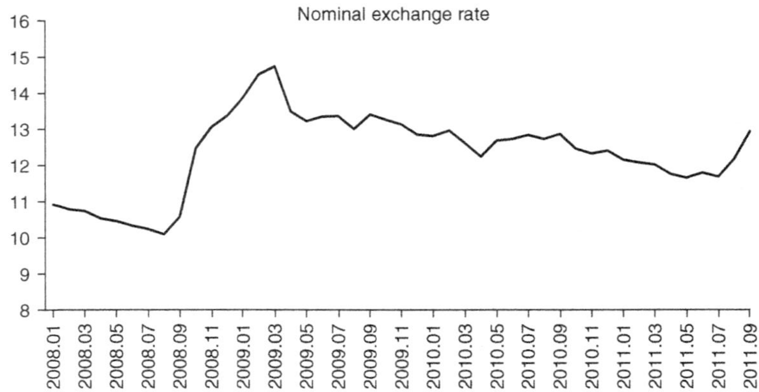

Figure 5.4 Mexico: Evolution of the Nominal Exchange Rate: 2008:01–2011:10 (pesos to the US dollar).

Note: Average exchange rate for the month.

Source: Banco de Mexico.

dollar in July 2008, the pressures in the foreign exchange market in the third quarter of 2008, derived from capital outflows and the shock to external demand, led to a rapid depreciation of the peso up until February 2009 when the exchange rate reached a peak of nearly 15 pesos per dollar (see Figure 5.4).[8] From March 2009, the Bank of Mexico took a series of measures to reverse the depreciation that took the peso in 2011 to a level of around 11 pesos per dollar before a new shock to the capital account led to a further depreciation of the peso in the second half of 2011. The real exchange rate followed closely, although to a lesser extent, the evolution of the nominal exchange rate. After the initial devaluation and subsequent recovery, the real exchange rate of the peso was in February 2011 at the level of January 2008.

The contrast between Canada and Mexico with respect to the evolution of the exchange rate is remarkable and probably explains why the recovery of the Canadian economy was slower than that of Mexico. Like the Mexican peso, the Canadian dollar depreciated during the "flight to quality" between October 2008 and April 2009. However, the depreciation of the Canadian dollar was much smaller (around the 20% instead of

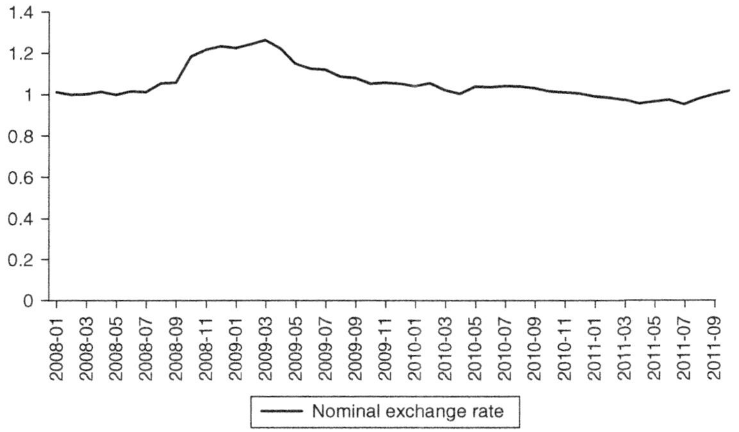

Figure 5.5 Canada: Evolution of the Nominal Exchange Rate: 2008:01–2011:10 (Canadian Dollars to the US Dollar).

Note: Average exchange rate for the month.

Source: Bank of Canada.

50% in the case of the Mexican peso) (Figure 5.5). The reason is that the impact of the "flight to quality" was much lower in the case of Canada as can also be seen in the evolution of the margin of sovereign risk. In addition, the subsequent appreciation that occurred in both cases led the Canadian dollar to the precrisis level (around 1 Canadian dollar per US dollar) during the first half of 2010. The Mexican peso, in contrast, never returned to its precrisis level (10 pesos per dollar) and eventually stabilized at around 13 pesos per US dollar (30% above the precrisis level). This contrast, which implied a significant difference in the evolution of the real exchange rates, probably explains why, as we saw in the second section, Canada's exports grew less than those of Mexico in the recovery phase. This is the factor that explains why the recovery in the level of economic activity in Canada was slower than in Mexico. Paradoxically, the greater financial-economic strength of Canada prevented the real exchange rate from playing more fully the role of an automatic stabilizer as happened in Mexico, an economy more vulnerable and less solid financially.

CONCLUSIONS

We saw in this chapter that the expectations of huge static and dynamic benefits from the economic integration of North America were very far from being fulfilled even though, as anticipated, there was a very strong expansion of trade in the area and some acceleration of foreign investment flows among the three economies involved in the NAFTA. This is especially true in the case of Mexico, with a developing economy that features much lower real wages and levels of productivity and per capita incomes equivalent to a quarter of the levels prevailing in its NAFTA trading partners. These disparities in real wages and productivity levels were, in the eyes of many analysts of the NAFTA, great opportunities for economic convergence among the trading partners of the treaty. In reality, far from the expected convergence of real wages, productivity levels, and per capita incomes what has tended to happen is a process of divergence in these variables.

The analysis of the external and internal factors in the crisis and recession of 2008–2009 pointed toward the role of the economic policy response in the explanation of the comparative behavior of aggregate economic activity in the two countries. This role of the internal response can be illustrated by the fact that, as we have seen, the fiscal stimulus package was much higher in Canada than in Mexico (4.1% vs. 1.3% of GDP) and the reduction of the Central Bank interest rate target was also more pronounced in Canada.

Just as the recession was more severe in Mexico than in Canada, due to the use of more determined countercyclical policies in the latter case, the recovery was faster in Mexico. This is attributable, as we have seen, to the dynamic behavior of Mexican exports that contrasts with the slow expansion of Canadian exports. Behind this different behavior is the contrast in the evolution of the real exchange rate which depreciates in the case of Mexico (severely up to March/April 2009) and appreciates in the case of Canada (from the beginning of 2009).

This contrast in turn is linked to the fact that the shock to the capital account, derived from the "flight to quality" unleashed by the collapse of Lehman Brothers, is much larger in the case of Mexico. Thus, although Mexico had a fiscal and monetary policy less countercyclical than Canada, the real exchange rate acted as an automatic stabilizer (the only one available to the economy) that allowed the early and vigorous export recovery. The result is that, comparing the level of GDP in the third quarter of 2011 with the first quarter of 2008, the two economies were in exactly the same situation with a GDP that was approximately 2% above its precrisis level (see Figure 5.3). A similar comparison by *The Economist*[9] magazine shows that per capita GDP in the second quarter of 2011 was 1% below the level of the last quarter of 2007 in the two countries (compared with 3% down in the case of the United States). In contrast, the per capita GDP of several countries was higher than the precrisis level, such as China (35%), India (22%), Argentina (17%), and Brazil (10%). In several other countries per capita GDP was still far below the precrisis level. Such is the case of Ireland (–12%), Greece (–11%), and Spain (–6%).

6

Why Does the Mexican Economy Grow Less Than That of Chile?

Chile and Mexico represent two extreme cases of economic growth performance in the past few decades in Latin America. The first one is considered to be a successful case, if not the most successful, of economic development in the region whereas the second one presents one of the economies that grows at a very slow pace in Latin America leading to all kinds of speculations on what has failed in the transformation of its economic development strategy.

This chapter addresses the question of why the Mexican economy grows less than that of Chile? I start with some of the long-term growth stylized facts in both countries. Then, I briefly review the processes of economic liberalization and international integration to emphasize the great convergence of both cases. Then, I consider if the accumulation of human capital is what explains the growth differential. Finally, I emphasize the main differences in macroeconomic policies that, in my view, are the source of the divergent performance in the two countries, as well as the role of China in the 2000s as an important importer of commodities exported by Chile and a formidable exporter of manufactures that compete with those that Mexico produces.

The Stylized Facts of Long-term Growth

Table 6.1 shows the long-term rates of growth of Mexico and Chile since 1950 and some other indicators closely linked to

Table 6.1 Chile and Mexico: Growth Rates of GDP Per Capita, Capital Stock Per Worker, Industrial Output, and Labor Productivity in Manufacturing and Services in 1950–1981, 1981–1990, and 1990–2011

Annual growth rates Mexico/Chile	1950–1981	1981–1990	1990–2011
Per capita GDP	3.3/1.6[1]	-1.0/0.9	1.2/4.0
Capital per worker	4.3/2.1	-0.7/-1.6	1.9/4.3
Industrial output	7.6/4.4	1.9/2.5	2.6/3.9
Labour productivity in manufacturing	2.5/3.9	-1.1/-2.1	1.7/3.7
Labour productivity in services	1.6/1.0	-2.5/-2.2	0.1/1.1

[1] 1951–1981.

Sources: André Hofman provided the estimates of capital stocks. Value added, employment and labour productivity are based on Timmer and de Vries (2007). The information of employment and value added were extrapolated to 2011 with different sources.

growth performance. As can be seen in the table, the Mexican economy grew more than the Chilean one between 1950 and the debt crisis of the 1980s, a feature that is reversed since the 1980s when Chile grows significantly more than Mexico. This situation is generally interpreted by saying that Mexico was one of the winners during the period of state-led industrialization whereas Chile was one of the losers and, on the other hand, one of the major winners in the period of economic liberalization and external opening.

Figures 6.1 and 6.2, which show the trend of GDP and its fluctuations in both countries since 1950, confirm the remarkable break in the trend of GDP growth in Mexico since the beginning of the 1980s.[1] It is worth noting the absence of a similar break in the case of the Chilean economy suggesting that, at least in terms of total GDP, there is not a much better performance of the Chilean economy in the second period compared to the first one.

This reversal of fortune in terms of growth performance is accompanied by other changes. The rate of accumulation of capital per worker, industrial output growth, the growth of manufacturing and services productivity are all lower in Mexico than in Chile in 1990–2011 after having been higher in the years 1950–1981 (with the exception of manufacturing productivity).

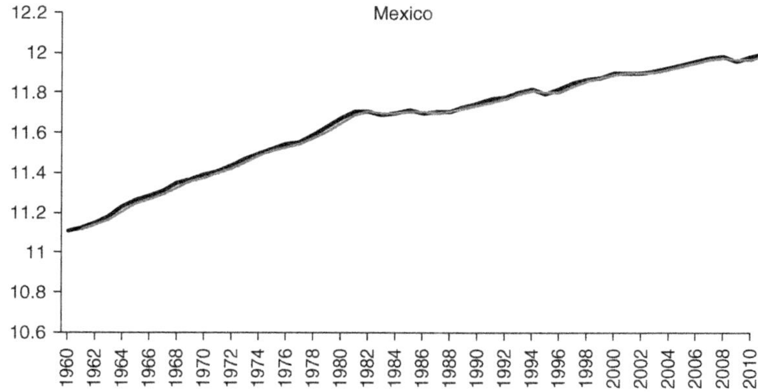

Figure 6.1 Mexico: GDP and Its Trend (logarithms).
Source: World Development Indicators.

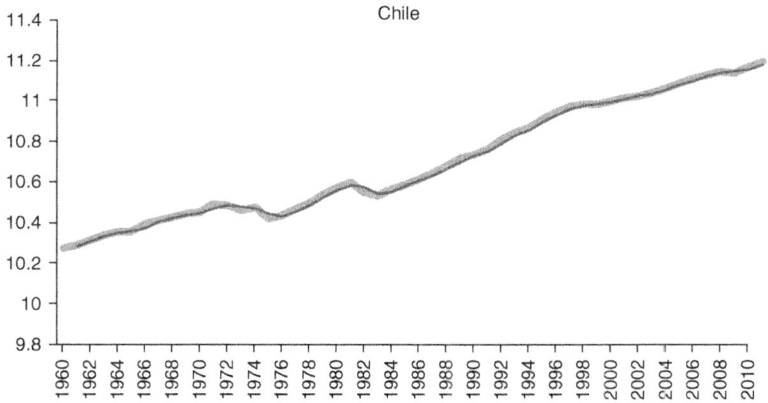

Figure 6.2 Chile: GDP and Its Trend (logarithms).
Source: World Development Indicators.

It is worth noting also that growth performance during the adjustment to the debt crisis was much better in Chile than in Mexico. Colombia and Chile are exceptions to the brutal contraction of GDP per capita growth in Latin America during the lost decade. As Fanelli et al. (1993) argued a long time ago, this is because in the case of Colombia this country was a minor debtor who did not suffer to the same extent as other debtor

Table 6.2 Growth Decomposition in Chile and México from 1990 to 2011

Annual Growth Rates	Output Per Worker	Capital Per Worker	TFP (Total Factor Productivity)
Chile	2.2	3.6	0.2
México	0.8	1.6	–0.2

Source: Feenstra, Robert C., Robert Inklaar, and Marcel P. Timmer (2013), "The Next Generation of the Penn World Table" available for download at www.ggdc.net/pwt.

countries did from the debt crisis of the 1980s and, in the case of Chile, because this country was a debtor that recovered very soon from the recession induced by the crisis, largely because of the availability of multilateral financing that made possible large deficits in the current account of the balance of payments. These two countries, Colombia and Chile, are practically the only ones among the major economies of Latin America where output growth exceeded 2% per year in the lost decade (see chapter 1).

It is also worth noticing, in the growth decomposition exercise for the period 1990–2011 which is presented in Table 6.2, that the difference in output per worker growth rates is attributable for the most part to the difference in the rates of capital accumulation per worker (a difference of 2 percentage points per year) since the performance of total factor productivity is poor in both countries (and the difference between the two is only 0.4 percentage points).

Market Reforms and Economic Performance

What is the reason for the better performance of Chile since 1990? In this section I argue that in terms of microeconomic reforms in the areas of foreign trade, privatization of public enterprises and flexibility of the labor market there has been a great convergence between the two countries.

As can be seen in Table 6.3 trade reform has been deep in both cases. The average tariff on imports fell from similar levels

Table 6.3 Openness to Foreign Trade

Average Tariff (%)	1985	2010
Chile	36	4
Mexico	34	6
Foreign trade as % of GDP	**1980**	**2008**
Chile	49.3	85.7
México	28.4	58.8

Source: Based on World Bank, World Development Indicators and Penn World Table 8.0.

in 1985 (around 35%) to 4% in Chile and 6% in Mexico in 2010. Moreover, having a free trade agreement with the trading partner that concentrates more than 80% of its exports it could be argued that trade liberalization has gone further in Mexico than in Chile. In any case, the process led to a sharp increase in the share of foreign trade to GDP in the two countries and the fact that this share is greater in Chile (85.7%) than in Mexico (58.8%) should probably be attributed to the fact that being a smaller economy, Chile tends as other small economies to be more specialized and present a higher foreign trade coefficient.

Data on privatization of public enterprises is dispersed and unfortunately there are few internationally comparable data of the share of public enterprises. The World Bank (1995), in the most complete existing work, has data until 1991. The Fraser Institute's data, which are shown in Table 6.4, measure the importance of public enterprises by the share of its sales in GDP but have several shortcomings mentioned by Ocampo and Malagón (2011), such as the fact that the statistics do not come from a single source and they are not necessarily consistent over time or internationally comparable. In any case, these data indicate that the process of privatization of public enterprises has been profound in the two countries taking the size of the public sector in 2005 well below the average for Latin America or Asia. In Chile this size went from a peak of 77% of GDP in 1975 to a minimum of 12.7% in 2005 while

Table 6.4 Participation of Public Companies in Economic Activity (% the GDP)

Year	Chile	Mexico	Latin America	Asia	Developed
1970	42.1	33.3	30.4	37.0	34.3
1975	77.0	40.2	34.0	39.5	31.7
1980	32.2	43.5	38.4	43.2	29.7
1985	16.1	38.0	35.4	42.9	29.1
1990	20.5	23.2	30.2	37.1	28.6
1995	16.6	19.6	26.1	27.3	24.3
2000	28.2	15.0	23.1	33.7	22.0
2005	12.7	19.7	23.9	29.8	13.4

Source: Ocampo and Malagón (2011) based on Fraser Institute.

in Mexico it went from 43.5% in 1980 to a minimum of 15% in 2000.

In the area of the labor market, Chile introduced several reforms since the period of the military dictatorship while Mexico just did in 2012. However, as I have argued elsewhere (Ros, 2013a), Mexico has a relatively flexible labor market when we take into account the value of the minimum wage (more than three times lower than that of Chile), its high turnover rate or its low rate of unionization. It is only in the case of employment protection and nonwage labor costs that it has values exceeding those of Chile (Table 6.5). I might add that Mexico has a lower degree of effectiveness of the labor market legislation. Perhaps the best way to illustrate the distance between the "rigidity" of the legal framework and the real flexibility of the labor market is that, while Mexico has a higher rate of employment protection, the turnover rate is much higher than in Chile.

In sum, in relation to market-oriented reforms in the fields of foreign trade and the productive activity of the public sector the changes have been profound in the two countries while in the labor market the degree of flexibility does not look very different. It would thus seem that it is not here where we can find the reasons for the divergence in terms of growth between the two economies.

Table 6.5 Mexico and Chile: Indicators of Labor Market Rigidities

Indicator	Mexico	Chile	Source
ILO conventions[1]	78	61	ILO (NORMLEX)
Minimum wage (US dollars, 2011)	110	372	CEPAL (2014)
Labour protection (OCDE, 2008)	3.2/6	1.8/6	Venn (2009)
Turnover rate	c. 50%	c. 30%	Bensusán (2006)
Dismissal costs (2008)[2]	52.0	52.0	World Bank, Doing Business 2009
Unionization rate (c. 2010)	15%[4]	14.3[4]	Bensusán and Middlebrook 2012, Hayter and Stoevska 2011, Visser 2011
Non-wage labour costs	15.5[5]–23[6]	7[5]–21[6]	OECD 2011a Heckman and Pagés 2004
Cost of collective rights compliance	2.2	2.6	Bensusán (2006)
Indicators of aggregate labour rigidity			
Fraser Institute	5.5	5.3	Freeman 2010
World Bank[3]	31.9	24	World Bank, Doing Business 2009 and 2013

[1] Number of ILO conventions ratified.
[2] Weeks' wages.
[3] Based on World Bank (2009, 2013). This indicator was constructed as a simple average of the corresponding ratios for the ease of dismissal, ease of recruitment, rigidity of hours of work, relationship between minimum wage and value added per worker and firing costs. These last two were normalized using the maximum value of each of the variables in the sample of countries reported by the OECD.
[4] Percentage of the employed labor force.
[5] Percentage of total labour costs (2010).
[6] Social security contributions as percentage of wages (1998).

HUMAN CAPITAL AND GROWTH

To what extent human capital has been an important factor in the growth differential between Chile and Mexico in the last three decades? Human capital can influence economic growth in two ways. The first, which corresponds to the more conventional vision, refers to the human capital as a factor of production. If human capital enters the production function, along with the physical capital, labor and natural resources, then its accumulation over time will have the effect of expanding production. The second relates to human capital as a vehicle of technological diffusion, that is, the rate at which a country adopts and adapts the technologies of the technological leaders. In this vision, the true importance of education lays not so much in its direct contribution to production, but in its contribution to technological diffusion. In the first case, in the vision of human capital as a productive factor, the *pace of growth* of human capital affects the output growth rate. In the second case, in the vision of human capital as a vehicle of the technological diffusion, the *level* of human capital (or the level relative to that of the technological leaders) influences the rate of productivity growth.

Table 6.6 shows an index of human capital (based on average years of schooling and returns to education) and average years of schooling as well as the growth of these two indicators in the two countries since 1981. It is remarkable how, starting from a lower level of schooling, the accumulation of human capital, according to the two indicators, has been significantly faster in Mexico than in Chile so that toward the end of the recent period average years of schooling of the population over 25 years were very similar in the two countries (9.7 and 8.5 in Chile in Mexico respectively).

All this is not surprising. The phenomenon of a rapid accumulation of human capital in the midst of economic stagnation has been extensively documented in the case of Mexico. There are indeed unmistakable signs that in this case slow growth has restricted the use of human capital in production rather than the reverse. Information on unemployment rates and informal employment rates in different groups of workers classified by educational level shows an almost continuous increase since 1989 especially in the groups with high level of education (with secondary education and higher). A recent study of the professionals' labor market (Hernández Laos et al., 2013) shows that

Table 6.6 Chile and Mexico: Level and Accumulation of Human Capital

Level and Average Annual Growth Rates	Mexico 1981–1990	Mexico 1990–2011	Chile 1981–1990	Chile 1990–2011
Human capital index	2.04	2.46	2.50	2.77
(PWT 8.0)	(1.5)	(1.2)	(1.3)	(0.6)
Years of schooling	4.9	7.2	7.3	8.8
(Barro-Lee)	(3.2)	(2.2)	(2.3)	(1.0)

Annual growth rates in per cent are shown in parentheses.

Source: PWT 8.0 and Barro and Lee (2012).

the professional's unemployment rate (people with complete higher education) grew steadily from 2000 to 2009, and faster than the overall unemployment rate.[2] In the case of professionals under the age of 25 the unemployment rate almost doubled from 7.8% in 2000 to 13.5% in 2009. These trends do not seem to be the result of a growing mismatch between the composition of supply and the requirements of the productive apparatus since the phenomenon is widespread. As shown in the same study mentioned above, in only six out of 45 careers more than 75% of the net supply of professionals obtained employment in occupations consistent with their university training while in 35 of the 45 less than half did it. The latter include all the engineering professions in addition to agronomy, marine sciences, and ecology (see Hernández Laos et al., 2013, p. 258).[3] Another sign of the underemployment of human capital is the significant increase in the emigration of skilled workers. According to the study of Hernández Laos et al. (2013), the professionals who migrated to the United States between 1998 and 2009 accounted for 8% of the graduates of higher education during 2001–2009, a significant increase compared to the previous decade (5.9% of the graduates of higher education between 1991 and 2000). According to another study (SELA, 2009), the dimension of the emigration of professionals is even greater: Mexico occupies the first place among the countries of Latin America and the Caribbean in the number of skilled workers who have migrated toward the OECD countries, with

1,357,000 graduates of bachelor, master or doctoral studies, approximately 16% of the total of Mexican professionals living within and outside the country in 2007.[4] In addition, Mexico is the country that recorded the fastest growing stock of skilled migrants between 1990 and 2007 (270%) in Latin America and the Caribbean (SELA, 2009).

With respect to the quality of education, international student evaluations show both Chile and Mexico very far from the educational international frontier and the differences between them do not seem to be significant enough to influence growth performance. Consider the results of the 2009 PISA test. The Mexican position (48) among the 65 countries that participated in the test places it only four places below Chile and both countries were better placed than the rest of the Latin American countries that participated in the test with the exception of Uruguay (i.e., three places above Mexico): below Mexico were Colombia (4 places), Brazil (5 places), Argentina (10 places), Panama (14 places) and Peru (15 places), these last three countries, by the way, with three of the highest growth rates in Latin America during the last decade. In the mathematics test, the result for Mexico (419) is virtually the same as for Chile (421), the leader among the Latin American countries that participated in the test, and both ratings are much lower than the OECD average (496).

The explanation of the paradox that the country with a faster accumulation of human capital is the one with the lowest growth has to do with demographic phenomena. When Mexico entered in the mid-1970s to the stage of the demographic transition toward low population growth with a changing age structure of the population in the direction of reducing the percentage of school-age population, the rate of human capital accumulation took off, like in other Latin American countries with rapid industrialization and high population growth until the early 1970s. But this is the period that witnessed the debt crisis of the 1980s that wreaked havoc with output growth, followed by a disappointing growth performance during the postmarket reforms period. Where this did not happen is precisely in those countries such as Chile that improved their economic performance after 1990 (in relation to the period of industrialization) and at the same time recorded relatively low rates of accumulation of human capital (in relation to their historical rates) in part because the benefits of the demographic bonus had already been exhausted. These interactions between demographics, human capital progress, and the characteristics of productive performance explain the paradox that the rate of accumulation of human capital is negatively correlated with economic growth. In any case, we cannot attribute to a higher level of human capital in Chile or to a more rapid accumulation of this factor in that country the fact that its economy has grown faster than that of Mexico: the accumulation of human capital has been faster in Mexico and the levels of human capital have tended to converge.

Macroeconomic Policy and Growth

If microeconomic reforms and human capital accumulation are not the factors that explain the difference in growth between the two countries, let's see now if we can find the explanation of that difference in macroeconomic policies.

Investment in Infrastructure

One of the legacies of the adjustment to the debt crisis in Mexico was a brutal contraction (of nearly 7 percentage points of GDP) of public investment, including investment in infrastructure that was one of the main victims. As a result, in the period 2001–2006 public investment in infrastructure had fallen to only 0.5% of GDP almost 2 percentage points of GDP below the level of 1981–1986, a level surely already depressed by the fiscal adjustments of the beginning of the 1980s (Table 6.7). Chile's experience was very different. Although public investment in infrastructure also fell between

Table 6.7 Investment in Infrastructure (percentage of the GDP)

	Total		Public		Private	
	1981–1986	2001–2006	1981–1986	2001–2006	1981–1986	2001–2006
Chile	3.4	5.2	3.4	1.7	0.0	3.5
Mexico	2.4	1.2	2.4	0.5	0.0	0.7

Source: Calderón and Serven (2011).

1981–1986 and 2001–2006, it did starting from higher levels than in Mexico (3.4 instead of 2.4 percentage points of GDP) and to a lesser extent. In addition, this fall was more than offset by a strong increase of 3.5 percentage points of GDP in private investment in infrastructure. In Mexico, by contrast, the small increase (0.7 percentage points of GDP) in private investment in infrastructure was very far from compensating the sharp decline in public investment. As a result of all this Mexico invested in infrastructure 4 percentage points of GDP less than Chile in 2001–2006.

This difference in investment in infrastructure is reflected in the evolution of the infrastructure stocks in the two countries. Available estimates of the infrastructure stocks show that between 1990 and 2005 while this stock quadrupled in the case of Chile, it did not even double in the case of Mexico (Perrotti and Sánchez, 2011). This was also reflected in the evolution of the quality of infrastructure. The available indicators of infrastructure quality (WEF) in 2010–2011 put Chile ranking 24 among 139 countries and Mexico ranking 79. In all the subindices of infrastructure quality from roads quality up to mobile telephony lines, Chile appears better placed than Mexico with the single exception of railway infrastructure quality where both are poorly ranked (77 and 76, respectively).

Although it is not possible to quantify what impact these differences have on growth performance in the two countries, it is possible that the effect is considerable. Indeed, the available estimates for Latin America show that the impact of infrastructure on growth can be very important. Calderón and Servén (2011) estimate that the growth of Latin America would increase by approximately 2 percentage points per year if the level of infrastructure development of each Latin American country reached the average level in the non-Latin-American-middle-income countries.

The Real Exchange Rate

Table 6.8 shows the evolution of the real exchange rate in two full economic cycles in the two countries over the 1990s and 2000s. The real exchange rate used shows the degree of undervaluation (a higher index indicates a more depreciated real exchange rate) and is estimated in a way that is comparable among countries.[5] Three observations follow from the table. The first is that in the first economic cycle of the 1990s (1992–1998 in Chile and 1994–2000 in Mexico), the Chilean average rate of growth exceeded by far the Mexican one although the degree of exchange undervaluation was very similar in the two countries. This is the period in which the Mexican peso was for several years very undervalued in the wake of the financial crisis of 1994–1995 and when the average growth rate was heavily pushed down by the severe 1995 recession. If we exclude this recession (which meant a drop in GDP of around 5%) Mexico's growth rate would have been in this period of the order of 5% per year, much closer to the Chilean one than the one that took place of 3.5% per year.

Table 6.8 Growth and the Real Exchange Rate

Chile	1992–1998	1998–2007
GDP growth	6.7	4.1
Degree of undervaluation	0.15	0.04
Mexico	1994–2000	2000–2011
GDP growth	3.5	2.0
Degree of undervaluation	0.17	-0.08

Source: Based on PWT 8.0.

The second observation is that in the second full cycle the growth differential in favor of Chile is in part associated with a significant difference in the degree of exchange undervaluation rate in favor of that country. In the case of Mexico, Blecker (2009) estimates that the real appreciation of the Mexican peso (an appreciation of the order of 10%) between 1996–2000 and 2003–2007 reduced the rate of growth as much as 1.3 percentage points (more than half of what the growth rate fell, approximately from 5% in the first period to 3% in the second).[6] The third observation is that there has been a trend of the real exchange rate toward appreciation in the two countries in the 1990s and 2000s that has been accompanied by a slowdown in growth in the two cases. This trend to real exchange rate appreciation is clearly visible in Figures 6.3 and 6.4.

All this suggests that the level of the exchange rate has had a significant role in the explanation of the growth differential

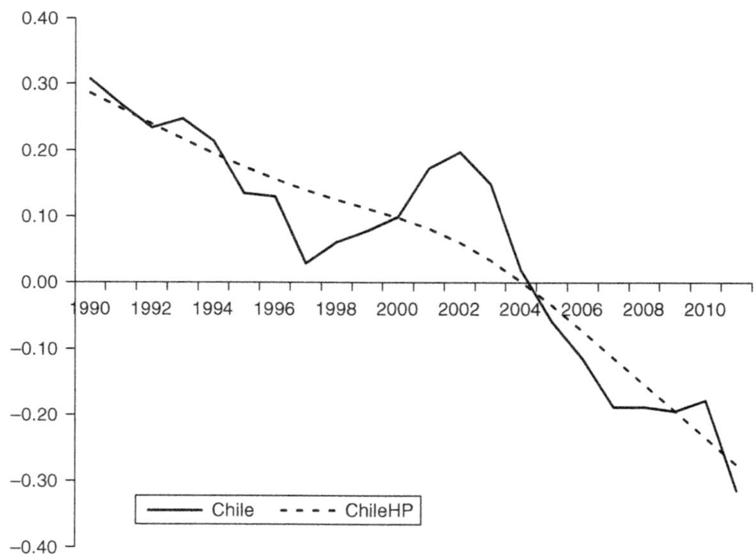

Figure 6.3 Chile: Real Exchange Rate and Its Trend.

Source: Feenstra, Robert C., Robert Inklaar and Marcel P. Timmer (2013), "The Next Generation of the Penn World Table" available for download at www.ggdc.net/pwt.

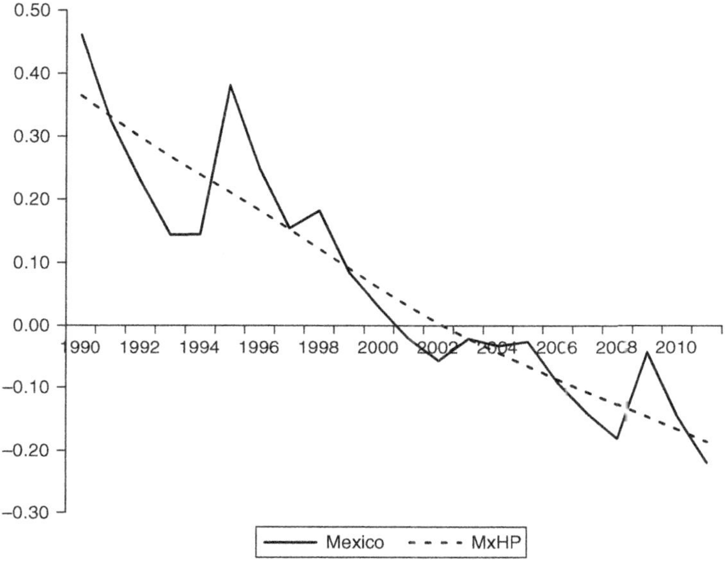

Figure 6.4 Mexico: Real Exchange Rate and Its Trend.

Source: Feenstra, Robert C., Robert Inklaar and Marcel P. Timmer (2013), "The Next Generation of the Penn World Table" available for download at www.ggdc.net/pwt.

between the two countries and the tendency to the slowdown in growth in both cases. How to explain the trend toward real exchange rate appreciation in the two cases? Elsewhere I have argued that monetary policy, under the inflation-targeting regime adopted by the two countries, has tended to be asymmetric in the face of changes in the exchange rate (Galindo and Ros, 2008; Ros, 2013a). Figure 4.9 in chapter 4 shows the evolution of the real exchange rate in several countries in Latin America aggregated in three groups according to their monetary policy regime (inflation targeting with floating exchange rate regimes, dollarized regimes, and others). As shown in the figure, the trend toward real exchange rate appreciation in the period 2002–2013 is more pronounced in countries with inflation targeting regimes than in the other two groups of countries. This is so especially for the period 2002–2008 before the fight to quality in the third quarter of 2008 and the ensuing depreciation. All this suggests that under inflation targeting exchange-rate shocks that tend to depreciate the currency and to increase the price level have been faced with restrictive monetary policies (increase in interest rates)—precisely in order to halt the inflationary impact of the devaluations—while shocks that tend to appreciate the exchange rate and to reduce inflation have not been faced with analogous expansionary monetary policies.

In the case of Mexico, to explain why the monetary and exchange rate policy has a bias toward exchange rate appreciation it is enough to recognize two features of the Mexican economy. First, under an inflation-targeting regime (especially in its strict version, which means that the central bank will react only to changes in the price level) monetary policy focuses on achieving a low inflation using the interest rate as the main policy instrument while it ignores other policy goals such as employment and growth. Given the high degree of openness to foreign trade in the economy and, as a result, the relatively strong impact of the exchange rate on the price level (in relation to the impact of the interest rate that operates on the components of aggregate demand which are interest-rate sensitive), it becomes very tempting for central banks to subordinate the exchange rate to their inflation targets or respond in a way that is not symmetrical to appreciations and depreciations.[7] There has been as a result a "fear to depreciate"—more than a "fear of floating"—in the face of external shocks, which tends to make monetary policy procyclical.[8] For example, in the face of a negative demand shock on our exports, which has a recessionary impact, the monetary authority tends to moderate the pressure toward depreciation of the exchange rate through an increase in the interest rate, which deepens the recession. This is what happened in the recession of 2001–2002 and again in 2008.

Second, due to low development of credit markets, the sensitivity of aggregate demand to movements in the interest rate is low and therefore, in these conditions, central banks may need to raise excessively the interest rate to achieve its inflation target. The high interest rates attract external capital flows, which in turn tends to appreciate the exchange rate This pro-appreciation bias of monetary policy is not unique to Mexico in Latin America, as we have seen. It is shared by all countries of Latin America with an inflation-targeting regime such as Brazil, Chile, Colombia, and Peru, which strongly suggests that the problem is with this monetary policy regime.

Bank Credit and Real Interest Rate

The lack of bank finance for productive activities has received an increasing attention in Mexico as a factor that has restricted investment in recent decades. As illustrated in Figure 6.5 in this aspect the situation differs considerably from that prevailing in Chile. While in Mexico bank credit to the private sector collapsed after the crisis of 1994–1995 reaching 20% of GDP in

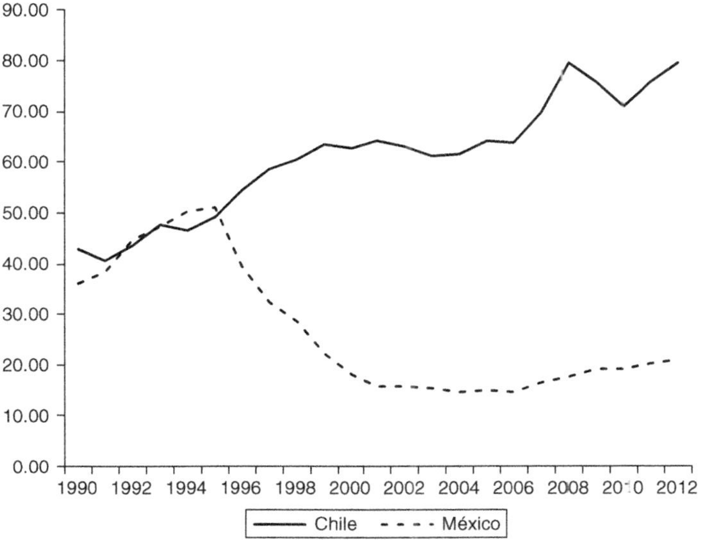

Figure 6.5 Bank Credit to the Private Sector, Balances at the End of the Period (% of GDP)

Source: Central Bank of Chile, Carlos Salinas de Gortari's Sixth Government Address, Banco de México, and INEGI.

2012 after a slight recovery since the middle of the first decade of 2000s, in Chile bank credit expanded considerably from levels similar to those of Mexico in the early 1990s and reaching 80% of GDP in 2012, four times Mexico's level.

In addition, Mexico's banking system features a lower level of operating efficiency than Chile's while at the same time having higher profitability. As shown in Table 6.9 the operating costs are almost 30% higher than in Chile while financial profitability is more than 20% higher than that of the Chilean banking

Table 6.9 Efficiency and Performance of the Banking System, 2005

Country	Operating Costs[1]	Financial Profitability[2]
Mexico	3.7	20.5
Chile	2.9	16.9

[1] Average ratio of operating costs/assets.
[2] Average ratio of after-tax returns /capital.
Source: Based on Chiquiar and Francia (2009).

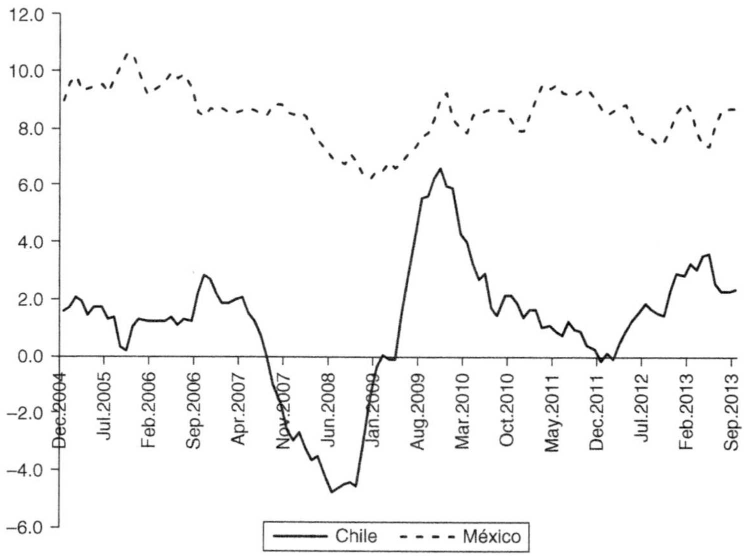

Figure 6.6 Real Interest Rate on Mortgages
Source: Banco Central de Chile and Banco de México.

system. There seems to be no doubt that, unlike what happens in Chile, in the Mexican banking sector the low efficiency, the high profit margins, and the high interest rates affect the general conditions of aggregate investment and, therefore, have, together with the shortage of bank credit, an adverse effect on economic growth. As shown in Figure 6.6, the real interest rate on mortgages is much higher in Mexico than in Chile in 2004–2013, the period for which we have comparable data.

Short-Run Fiscal Policy and Growth Volatility

A well-known difference between Mexico and Chile refers to the fiscal policy rule followed by the government. While in Chile the fiscal policy objective is determined as a structural surplus of 1% of GDP that gives room for a neutral or even countercyclical fiscal policy in the short run, in Mexico the government has been following a balanced budget rule (de jure since the 2006 fiscal responsibility law and de facto for decades now) that involves a procyclical fiscal policy. In Chile, for example, the structural surplus rule of 1% of GDP allowed between 2001 and 2007 an accumulation of reserves that reached 20% of GDP. In this way, in 2008, at the beginning of the crisis, the government could use them to introduce a large fiscal stimulus. In the case of Mexico, the procyclical nature of fiscal policy has been documented by several authors. Pastor and Villagómez (2007), for example, illustrate the procyclical behavior of fiscal policy since 1990 showing how the structural balance of the public sector[9] increases in years of recession (1995 for example) and decreases during periods of expansion (1992–1994 and 1999–2000).[10] The increase in the structural balance in times of recession, when government revenues are falling, implies that the government is reducing spending precisely when the level of economic activity is shrinking. This behavior reinforces the negative effects of a shock on the level of economic activity because at times of recession, when government revenues fall, the government cuts expenditure in order to maintain a balanced budget, which deepens the recession.

The difference between the two countries can be illustrated with some regression exercises. A first exercise for the period 1990–2008 takes as a dependent variable the adjustment of primary public spending (its growth with a negative sign to express its contribution to the improvement of the fiscal balance) and as an independent variable the growth of GDP and, alternatively, its cyclical component. The resulting elasticity of the primary fiscal adjustment vis-a-vis GDP measures how much public spending increases when GDP grows a percentage point above its trend and can be: (1) less than –1 in which case fiscal policy is procyclical (spending increases when the GDP grows above its trend); (2) between 0 and –1, in which case fiscal policy is noncyclical; or (3) greater than zero in which case fiscal policy is anticyclical (spending falls when GDP grows above its trend). As can be seen in lines 2 and 3 of Table 6.10 while Chile's fiscal policy falls into the category that we defined as noncyclical, Mexico's is strongly procyclical, even more than the average for Latin America. The table also shows the estimates of Suescún (2007) of the cyclical behavior of the fiscal balance. A positive sign in the regression suggests that a positive output gap is associated with an improvement of the fiscal balance. In this way, an economic expansion would be related to a lower fiscal deficit indicating that fiscal policy is anticyclical. The results show, again, that while Chile has a coefficient very close to 0 that suggests a noncyclical fiscal policy, Mexico's suggests a very procyclical policy.

This difference explains why, according to the OECD, deviations of GDP with respect to its trend have been higher in

Table 6.10 Regressions of Fiscal Adjustment and Fiscal Balance (vis-a-vis the cyclical component of GDP)

Elasticity	Chile	Mexico	Latin America	Developed
Cyclical component of the GDP	–0.43	–2.09	–1.99	
GDP growth	–0.50	–1.82	–1.54	
Cyclicity (Suescún, 2007)	–0.09	–0.40	–0.25	0.07

Source: Based on Ocampo and Malagón (2011).

Mexico than in most other OECD countries, including during the recent crisis. By exacerbating the economic cycle, a procyclical fiscal policy has adverse consequences on long-term growth because macroeconomic volatility is costly in terms of growth. First, it tends to reduce the rate of investment as it increases uncertainty and drives economic agents to prefer "defensive" microeconomic strategies that prevent compromising fixed capital in the productive process. At the same time, it skews the loans from the banking system toward shorter time horizons, as a result of the higher levels of risk faced by domestic financial systems. In addition, if a higher volatility translates into a lower degree of capacity utilization, this means not only that the level of well being of the population does not reach its full potential, but also slows down investment projects, by reducing profitability, and therefore, the rate of growth of the economy. On the other hand, human capital accumulation is adversely affected. Deep and extended recessions makes workers lose work experience and connections, while children and teenagers drop out of school and do not necessarily return later when the economy recovers (Lustig, 2000; Ocampo, 2003). All this implies irreversible losses of productive capacity. The empirical evidence shows that there is a strong negative correlation between procyclical fiscal behavior and long-term growth in a large sample of developing countries (United Nations, 2006).

The China Factor

Finally I should add that the emergence of China in the global economy as a formidable exporter of manufactured goods and huge importer of raw materials also seems to have contributed in the 2000s to explain the growth differential between Chile, supplier and exporter of raw materials to China, and Mexico, exporter of manufactures and competitor of China in the North American market. As a result China has become the main trading partner of Chile in Asia and the main competitor of Mexico in the North American market for manufactured goods. This

Table 6.11 Terms of Trade, Exports, and GDP in Chile and Mexico, 2000–2012 (Annual Growth Rates)

	Terms of trade 2008 (index 2000 = 100)	Exports volume	Exports value	GDP
Chile	164.7	4.1	12.5	4.1
Mexico	105.8	3.1	6.9	2.2

Source: World Bank, World Development Indicators.

has meant growth rates of the volume and value of exports in Chile higher than in Mexico (Table 6.11) and an increase in the terms of trade of Chile, which is the highest among the major Latin American economies.

CONCLUSIONS

To conclude, Mexico and Chile show important differences in the macroeconomic policy framework such as the level of investment in infrastructure, the level of the real exchange rate, and how it is affected by monetary and exchange rate policy, the regulation of the financial system and the degree to which it complies with its intermediary role, and the degree to which the fiscal policy helps to stabilize the level of economic activity through its anticyclical action. And these differences seem to explain much of the differential of growth between the two countries. To these, on should add the emergence of China in the 2000s as a major trading partner of Chile and a chief competitor of Mexico.

7

Mexico—Looking Ahead: Macroeconomic Policy and Development Strategy

As we have seen in chapter 5, the recession of 2008–2009 in Mexico was followed by a vigorous recovery in the third and fourth quarters of 2009. However, in the absence of a number of policy reforms the economy has returned in 2013 and 2014 to the lackluster growth performance that characterized the years 2000 to 2007 (when the growth rate of GDP averaged 2.4% per year).

In the current strategy for putting the Mexican economy on a path of high and sustained growth, the emphasis has been placed on microeconomic reforms in the areas of the labor market, the energy sector, competition policy, and others (see SHCP, 2010a, pp. 6 and 7, for the government's reform agenda). In this view, macroeconomic policy reforms are hardly mentioned (with the exception of tax reform). It would appear that in this approach all that macroeconomic policy can do to foster growth is to control inflation and thus, even when inflation is low, its control must be its main if not its only objective. Thus, with macroeconomic stability (narrowly defined as low and stable inflation) having been achieved, there is little, if anything, that macroeconomic policy can do to accelerate growth.

While microeconomic reforms in a number of areas are desirable in their own right it is doubtful that the disappointing growth performance in recent decades is due to the lack of these reforms as often asserted (for a discussion of this point see Ros, 2008, 2013a; Moreno-Brid and Ros, 2009, ch. 10). Thus, the currently dominant view fails to recognize that the lackluster growth performance of recent decades has macroeconomic roots and that greater emphasis should be put on the need to reform macroeconomic policies in order to provide a more growth-oriented macroeconomic framework. This need is also the conclusion that emerges from chapter 6 and the comparison of the growth performances of Chile and Mexico.

Growth, Public Investment, Procyclical Fiscal Policy, and Exchange Rate Appreciation

A solid diagnostics of the lack of growth in the Mexican economy must start by recognizing that the productivity growth slowdown that "explains," in a growth accounting sense, the growth slowdown of the Mexican economy in recent decades is largely an endogenous phenomenon, determined by the lack of growth itself and the resulting expansion of employment in the low productivity sectors of the economy (see Ros, 2008, 2013a; Moreno and Ros, 2009, ch. 10). Rather than an exogenous productivity growth deceleration, the proximate determinant of slow growth is the low rate of physical capital formation which fell from 7.3% per year in 1960–1981 to 4.0% in 1990–2008, being only 3.5% for the period 1981–2008 as a whole.[1] The inability of capital formation to grow at a fast pace—after the years of decline during the debt crisis—has prevented the expansion of employment in high productivity sectors and the modernization of productive capacity while at the same time constraining the growth of aggregate demand.

In turn, the proximate determinant of the reduction in the investment rate has been the contraction of public investment. As shown in Table 7.1, while total fixed investment fell by almost 5 percentage points of GDP between 1979–1981 and 2004–2007, public investment fell even more (collapsing

Table 7.1 Fixed Investment Rates (as a proportion of GDP)

	1979–1981	2004–2007	Difference
Total	24.9	20.0	-4.9
Private investment	13.9	15.6	1.7
Public investment	11.0	4.4	-6.6

Investment and GDP are at current prices.

Source: Based on INEGI, Sistema de Cuentas Nacionales.

by 6.6 percentage points). Whether there are crowding-out or crowding-in effects of public investment on private investment is subject to controversy (see, for opposite views, Lachler and Aschauer, 1998, which find a partial crowding-out effect, and Ramirez, 2004, which finds an important crowding-in effect). There is, however, consensus on the fact that, even if crowding-out effects exist, these are at worst partial, that is an increase in public investment increases total investment rather than displacing fully an equal amount of private investment. It follows that the decline in public investment is partly responsible for the fall in the overall investment rate and may even have had an adverse effect on private investment (if crowding in effects predominate).

The fall in public investment has partly to do with privatizations but also with the type of fiscal adjustment followed after the debt crisis. The macroeconomic adjustment followed was successful in correcting fiscal imbalances, in the sense of eliminating high and unsustainable public deficits, but it relied excessively on the contraction of public investment and failed dramatically in the task of strengthening nonoil tax revenues. As shown by Giugale et al. (2001), there is a close correlation since 1980 between fiscal deficit reductions and the fall in public investment (the correlation coefficient between the two turning out to be 0.82 between 1980 and 1997).

Infrastructure investment, which has the largest potential to affect productivity growth and private investment, has suffered in this contraction. In the period 2001–2006, Mexico, among the large Latin American economies with available information, was last in infrastructure investment as a fraction of GDP and this applied to both public and private investment (Table 7.2). During that period, as already mentioned in chapter 6, Mexico invested in infrastructure 4 percentage points of GDP less than Chile, the only country in Table 7.2 with an increase in infrastructure investment between 1981–1986 and 2001–2006. Mexico also stands out for having the largest contraction in infrastructure investment (50%) with the exception of Brazil. The fall in infrastructure investment took place in road construction, water provision, and electricity. Only in the case of telecommunications was there a recovery of investment in the 1990s. However, even in this case Mexico is today lagging behind other Latin American countries such as Chile and Brazil which were behind Mexico in 1980 (Calderón and Serven, 2004).

A second macroeconomic factor that constraints investment and growth is the tendency of fiscal policy to operate procyclically, as already pointed out in chapter 6. This has been amply illustrated by the available empirical studies. Pastor and Villagómez (2007) exemplify the procyclical behavior of fiscal policy during the period 1990–2003 showing how the structural balance of the public sector increases at time of recessions (1995 for example) and falls during expansions (1992–1994 and 1999–2000). Other studies finding a procyclical behavior

Table 7.2 Infrastructure Investment (percentage of GDP)

	Total		Public		Private	
	1981–1986	2001–2006	1981–1986	2001–2006	1981–1986	2001–2006
Chile	3.4	5.2	3.4	1.7	0.0	3.5
Colombia	3.1	2.8	3.1	1.7	0.0	1.1
Brazil	5.2	2.1	3.6	1.2	1.5	1.0
Peru	2.1	1.5	2.1	0.5	0.0	1.0
Argentina	2.8	1.7	2.8	0.7	0.0	1.0
Mexico	2.4	1.2	2.4	0.5	0.0	0.7

Source: Based on Calderón and Serven (2009).

of fiscal policy in Mexico are Talvi and Végh (2000), World Bank (2001), and Kaminsky et al. (2004).

The tendency has its origin in the procyclical behavior of capital markets and in a very low tax burden, which implies that public finances continue to be very vulnerable to changes in volatile oil revenues. Moreover, the balanced budget rule adopted in the fiscal responsibility law of 2006 has further accentuated the procyclical character of fiscal policy. As is well known, maintaining a constant fiscal deficit along the business cycle exacerbates the economic cycle since it ensures that the structural balance increases in recession years and falls during periods of expansion. Yet, this is the principle that has inspired fiscal policy management during the last several administrations and which has been institutionalized in the legislation on fiscal responsibility approved in 2006.

The procyclical behavior of fiscal policy exacerbates the negative effects of shocks to the level of economic activity and has adverse consequences on long-run growth. Indeed, a greater volatility of the level of economic activity, with the corresponding increase in uncertainty, reduces the rate of investment and modifies the composition of investment in favor of short-term investments (with negative effects on productivity growth) while deeper recessions can have irreversible adverse effects on learning by doing and workers skills.

The appreciation of the real exchange rate in 1988–1994 and later in the period 2000–2007 further conspired against investment in manufacturing and more generally in tradable goods sectors. While real exchange-rate appreciation can encourage fixed investment in developing countries by lowering the relative prices of imported machinery and equipment, it also shifts relative prices in favor of nontradable goods sectors, reducing the profitability of the tradable goods sectors and inhibiting capital accumulation in these activities. Blecker (2009) estimates that the real appreciation of the peso between 1996–2000 and 2003–2007 (a 9% appreciation) reduced Mexico's GDP growth rate by as much as 1.3 percentage points.[2] He also finds that an appreciated peso has had a more negative effect on growth since trade liberalization and especially since NAFTA took effect. Ibarra (2010) also finds a highly significant effect of the real exchange on investment even after controlling for industrial production and exports, suggesting therefore a very significant "profitability effect" of the real exchange rate.

The empirical evidence for other countries is also quite conclusive. Indeed, the relationship between the real exchange rate and growth has received much attention in recent years after the slow growth recorded by a large number of countries with overvalued real exchange rates and the extraordinarily high growth rates in countries that have deliberately undervalued their real exchange rate (this is the case of China and, in the Latin American context and to a lesser extent, of Argentina). As a result, there is today a large literature documenting a positive relationship between a high real exchange rate and growth (see chapter 3). In this recent literature, the effect of the real exchange rate on investment profitability, already mentioned, is the main but not the only mechanism through which the real exchange rate affects growth. The impact of investment on growth is amplified by the greater productivity of invested capital, mainly in sectors subject to international competition (Polterovich and Popov, 2002). Moreover, a high real exchange rate reallocates resources toward the tradable goods sectors, which present increasing returns to scale and whose expansion generates economies of specialization and technological externalities that are captured by the less dynamic sectors (Frenkel and Ros, 2006; Rodrik, 2008). Levy-Yeyati and Sturzenegger (2007) highlight the increase in domestic saving that results from the redistribution of income in favor of profits derived from a high real exchange rate. In small and medium-size firms with limited access to external finance, the resulting increase in internal funds has a positive effect on investment. The increase in overall savings also tends to reduce the cost of capital for large firms that finance their investments in the capital market.

Although macroeconomic factors are not the only determinants of slow growth—a more ample diagnostics should also refer to the role of industrial policy and the lack of bank finance for productive activities (see, on the subject, Moreno-Brid and Ros, 2009)—this analysis of the causes of slow growth in the Mexican economy suggests that a good deal of the economic policy agenda for growth should focus on the reform of macroeconomic policy.

THE REFORM OF MONETARY AND EXCHANGE RATE POLICY

Consider first monetary and exchange rate policy. The empirical evidence seems to suggest that Mexico's central bank has adopted a strict inflation targeting regime, focused exclusively on inflation targets, rather than a flexible framework that takes into account the output gap in the design of monetary policy (for a review of the evidence, see Esquivel, 2010). There is also some related evidence showing that monetary policy reacts asymmetrically to exchange rate shocks (tightening in the face of depreciations while not loosening enough in the face of appreciations) (Galindo and Ros, 2008).

If one accepts that price stability is consistent with multiple configurations of real wages, interest rates, and exchange rate, and that some of them are more favorable than others to economic growth, it follows that, without violating the constitutional mandate that requires the central bank to pursue price stability, monetary policy should seek such stability within the set of configurations favorable to growth.[3] Moreover, given that the configurations of relative prices that inhibit growth have often proven to be unsustainable, prudence dictates seeking price stability only within a context that is favorable to growth. There is thus a case for the flexibilization of the currently very strict inflation targeting framework and its combination with some form of real exchange rate targeting. Such flexibilization would contribute to resist the temptation to use the exchange rate as a counterinflationary policy instrument that is important to eliminating the tendency toward real currency appreciation and establishing a competitive real exchange rate. This requires systematically avoiding exchange rate overvaluation especially at times of recession; to avoid, that is, the implementation of a procyclical monetary policy such as the one followed in the early 2000s and again in the first semester of 2008 (see chapter 5). More precisely, the central bank could promote a competitive exchange rate by establishing a sliding floor to the exchange rate in order to prevent excessive appreciation (see Galindo and Ros, 2008). This would imply managing interest rates or intervening in the foreign exchange market at times when the exchange rate hits the floor but allow the exchange rate to float freely otherwise. Thus, under this alternative the central bank does not target a particular real exchange rate but only establishes a floor on it is value.

An objection to such a proposal is that by defending the floor the central bank loses control of the money supply and this could imply giving up the achievement of the inflation target (for a fuller discussion, see Frenkel and Rapetti, 2004). The problem arises at times of excess supply of foreign currency as a result, in particular, of massive capital inflows. It is worth noting, however, that speculative capital inflows will tend to be deterred to the extent that the central bank clearly signals that it will prevent the appreciation of the domestic currency thus stabilizing exchange rate expectations.[4]

TAX REFORM, PUBLIC INVESTMENT, AND FISCAL POLICY

Relaxing the constraints on public investment leads directly to the issue of tax reform and the mobilization of the fiscal space given by the low levels of public debt. Despite recent attempts at tax reform by the Fox, Calderón, and Peña Nieto administrations, nonoil tax revenues, at about 11% of GDP, continue to be extremely low by international standards, well below those prevailing in OECD countries and even below those of Latin American countries with similar per capita incomes (see OECD, 2007).

A priority area for investing the increased resources from a major tax reform is the development of the poor South. A "New Deal" that created the conditions to take advantage of the productive potential of the South, and to allow it to reach the medium development level of the rest of the country, would generate by itself a considerable additional impulse to the growth process, in addition to the reduction of regional inequalities. This requires eliminating and reverting the bias against these regions that most policies in the area of public capital or development incentives have shown so far. Infrastructure investment in these regions and the introduction of positive discrimination in their favor in other policies would open up new areas of investment and new markets thus liberating a growth potential that would contribute, for a considerable period, to a higher rate of growth of the economy as a whole (see, on the subject, Dávila et al. 2002). Although there are no estimates for Mexico, the available estimates for Latin America suggest that the effects can be considerable. Indeed, using a cross-country regression framework, Calderón and Servén (2011) estimate that growth in Latin America would increase by approximately 2 percentage points per year if the level of infrastructure development of each Latin American country were to rise to match the average level observed among non Latin American middle income countries.

Toward a Countercyclical Fiscal Policy

Another aspect of the reform of fiscal policy refers to its procyclical behavior. The most frequently given justification for the adoption of a fiscal policy that turns out to be procyclical focuses on the problems of credibility generated by governments that in the past were characterized by their "fiscal excesses." As discussed in Casar and Ros (2004), in the case of Mexico this argument seems an exaggeration after five six-year administrations in which the principal banner of economic policy has been the achievement of "healthy public finances." Moreover, even if the diagnosis of a lack of credibility was true, the response should be to establish credibility rather than to continue with a practice that contributes to deepen recessions. One can think for example of institutional arrangements—such as a multiyear fiscal rule with a ceiling to public indebtedness as a proportion of GDP—that guarantee the stability of public finances over the medium term without eliminating the room for maneuver for fiscal policy in the short run (for a proposal in this direction based on the adoption of a structural balance, see Pastor and Villagómez, 2007). The growth benefits of a countercyclical fiscal policy should not be underestimated as suggested by recent research (Aghion and Marinescu, 2006; Aghion et al., 2006) and its successful application in, for example, Chile, as discussed in chapter 6.

It is worth noting that both the IMF and the OECD are advocating a reform of the balanced budget rule. For example, in a recent article IV consultation, the IMF staff report states: "The balanced budget rule has been a key anchor, but there is a case for moving towards a structural rule over time. The current rule has built up the credibility of the fiscal framework. But moving to a structural rule would lower procyclicality and reduce the asymmetry inherent in the current framework" (IMF, 2010b, p. 32). Similarly, the OECD in the 2009 Economic Survey of Mexico states: "Fiscal policy is highly dependent on volatile oil income. The balanced budget rule can create a bias for spending oil revenues as they are earned, especially as transfers to the stabilization funds are limited by caps at low levels. This can potentially lead to a procyclical bias in fiscal policy.... To better manage budget cycles and oil wealth, Mexico should establish a structural deficit fiscal rule" (OECD, 2009a). The new government of President Peña Nieto is finally moving in this direction by abandoning the traditional fiscal rule in its 2014 budget.

IS THERE ANYTHING WRONG WITH MEXICO'S INSERTION INTO THE WORLD ECONOMY?

The emphasis on the low rate of investment in physical capital and the macroeconomic factors behind it as an explanation of Mexico's slow rate of economic growth in the postreform period suggests that other interpretations of Mexico's growth slowdown may be missing the point. In chapter 6, I have alluded to the allegedly incompleteness of microeconomic reforms as an explanation of Mexico's slow growth. This topic has also been addressed elsewhere (see Ros, 2008; Moreno and Ros, 2009, ch. 10; Ros, 2013a) where the argument is that the slow productivity growth rate, which is supposedly determined by the lack of microeconomic reforms, is in fact a consequence of the low rate of investment.

Consider now the question of the pattern of insertion of Mexico into the world economy. Mexico has integrated into the international economy as an exporter of not only oil but also of manufactured goods, both labor-intensive (garment and assembly of electronic products) and of medium and high technological intensity (automobiles, metal, and mechanical industries). Thus, the share of manufactures in total exports climbed from below 20% in the early 1980s to nearly 80% today at the expense of the share of oil exports, which fell from over two-thirds of the total in the early 1980s to less than 20% today. This transformation is remarkable in the international context. In the recent period, the manufacturing exports share in total exports is higher in Mexico than in several Latin American and East Asian countries (Table 7.3).

Moreover, manufacturing exports have a high share of consumer durable and capital goods with a high income elasticity of demand. And the technology intensity of Mexican exports has been increasing over time with the share of high-technology exports in total manufacturing exports reaching close to 20% by 2006 (see Table 7.4). Although lower than that of China, Malaysia, South Korea, and Thailand, this share is well above that

Table 7.3 Composition of Merchandise Exports (in percent of total)

	Argentina	Brazil	Chile	Indonesia	Korea	Malaysia	Mexico	Thailand
Manufactures								
1980	23.2	37.2	9.1	2.3	89.6	18.8	**11.9**	25.0
1993	31.9	58.9	16.5	53.1	93.1	69.7	**74.6**	71.1
2006	32.0	50.8	11.1	44.7	89.5	73.7	**76.0**	76.0
Agriculture[1]								
1980	71.2	50.3	24.9	21.7	8.8	46.0	**14.7**	57.1
1993	57.4	28.4	38.3	15.0	3.8	18.1	**8.5**	25.8
2006	46.4	28.7	20.5	18.1	1.6	9.7	**5.8**	16.6
Minerals and Oil[2]								
1980	5.7	11.2	65.4	75.8	1.3	34.9	**73.3**	13.9
1993	10.7	12.3	43.3	31.9	3.0	11.5	**16.5**	1.6
2006	20.2	18.5	66.4	37.2	8.5	15.1	**17.9**	6.2

[1] Food and agricultural raw material exports.
[2] Ore, metals and fuel exports.

Source: World Development Indicators (online).

Table 7.4 High Technology Exports (percentage of total manufacturing exports)

Mexico and Selected Developing Countries	1990	1997	2006
Malaysia	38.2	49.0	53.8
Korea	17.8	26.4	32.0
China	6.1 [1]	12.7	30.3
Thailand	20.7	30.7	27.3
Mexico	**8.3**	**17.5**	**18.9**
Brazil	7.1	7.3	12.1
Argentina	7.1 [1]	4.5	6.8
Chile	4.6	3.3	6.5

[1] 1992.

Source: Based on World Bank, World Development Indicators.

of Brazil, Argentina, and Chile. A significant share of medium and high technology-intensive exports has also been found in other studies for the Mexican case (Moreno-Brid et al., 2005; ECLAC, 2005).

It is also important to observe that among the major competitors in the US market, Mexico is the only one that has not suffered a major decline in its share in US imports in the face of the rapidly increasing participation of China (Table 7.5). In fact, despite a slight decline throughout the years 2000, Mexico's share in US imports was higher in 2001–2008 than in 1994–2000. This is in stark contrast with the decline of almost 6 percentage points in Japan's share or the fall of the order of 2 percentage points in Canada's share, the other major trading partners of the United States besides China and Mexico.

All this suggests that the pattern of integration into the world economy has not been a drag on Mexico's economic growth. In fact, the nature of Mexican exports should, if anything, have generated faster economic growth. Hausmann et al. (2005) show that the level of technological sophistication of a country's exports relative to its per capita income is a good predictor of a country's subsequent growth and it is clear from their findings that Mexico has a relatively high level of sophistication of its

Table 7.5 Share of US Imports (percentage)

	1990–1993	1994–2000	2001–2008	2008
China	4.3	7.1	13.5	16.1
Canada	18.8	19.4	17.3	16.0
Mexico	**6.4**	**9.6**	**10.8**	**10.3**
Japan	18.4	14.5	8.8	6.6
Germany	5.3	5.1	5.0	4.6

Source: Based on USITC data.

export basket, higher certainly than other Latin American economies with similar or even higher levels of income per capita (Chile and Argentina, for example). In other words, the Mexican economy has had a poor growth performance in recent decades despite a rather favorable pattern of trade specialization.

CONCLUSIONS

A growth diagnostics of the Mexican economy suggests that past development strategy has neglected the macroeconomic factors—such as a low public investment, a procyclical fiscal policy, and a tendency to the real appreciation of the peso—that are behind the lackluster growth of the economy in 2000s. A redirection of development strategy should thus consider the reform of macroeconomic policies as a central ingredient of the reforms necessary to put Mexico on a path of fast and self-sustained growth. This implies the mobilization of the fiscal space, including tax reform, necessary to recover high rates of public investment, the establishment of a competitive and stable real exchange rate, and the move toward a structural budget rule that allows fiscal policy to act countercyclically.

Notes

1 Institutional and Policy Convergence with Growth Divergence in Latin America

* Revised version of a paper prepared for the International Conference "Industrial Policies in the 21st Century" celebrating BNDES 60th Anniversary. I am grateful for excellent research assistance by Santiago Capraro, David Maldonado, and Luis Angel Monroy Gomez Franco.

1. This group of 20 countries includes those Latin American countries for which information is available in the Penn World Table. Table 1.1 shows these 20 countries.
2. Inflation targeting regimes now prevail in major Latin American countries. Chile and Colombia were the pioneers having adopted inflation targets since 1990 and 1991 respectively. Peru introduced a floating exchange rate regime in 1994 and in 2002 the central bank replaced quantitative targets for monetary aggregates with inflation targets using the interest rate as the main instrument of monetary policy. After the 1994–1995 crisis, Mexico let the peso float and in 1999 moved to an inflation targeting regime eventually adopting a target interest rate as policy instrument. Brazil also joined this group of countries in 1999 after the exchange rate crisis of the beginning of that year.
3. As shown in Table 1.6, Mexico is second only to Brazil in the rate of expansion of GDP although it is tied in fourth place behind Panama and Ecuador in terms of growth of output per capita.
4. Note that the rankings in Table 1.6 differ from those in Table 1.5, which uses the more appropriate concept for growth comparisons of GDP per person employed. Data for this is only available from 1980.

2 Productivity and Growth: Stylized Facts and Kaldor's Laws in Latin America

* This chapter is based in part on a study for the Economic Commission for Latin America and the Caribbean. I am grateful to Luis Angel Monroy Gómez Franco for excellent research assistance.

1. This literature starts with Romer (1986, 1990) and includes by now numerous contributions reviewed, among others, by Aghion and Howitt (2009).
2. For a detailed discussion, see Ros (2000, 2013b).
3. TFP growth rates are logarithmic and are based on the sources described in the Appendix.
4. Colombia and Chile are the exceptions because, in the first case, due to its low debt did not suffer as other countries did from the external debt crisis of the 1980s and, in the second case, because it recovered very rapidly from the recession caused by the crisis to a large extent due to the possibility of financing large current account deficits in the balance of payments with multilateral finance (World Bank and IMF) (see on the subject Fanelli et al., 1993). These are the only two countries where output growth exceeded 2% per year during the lost decade.
5. For an analysis of the views of Smith and Young together with those of Marshall and Kaldor, see Lavezzi (2001) on which I rely in this section.
6. Thus, in Smith, economic growth is associated with an increase in the complexity of economic activity, brought about by the division of labor: "It is the great multiplication of the production of all the different arts, in consequence of the division of labor, which occasions, in a well-governed society, that universal opulence which extends itself to the lowest ranks of people" (Smith, 1776, p. 9).
7. For Smith workers specialization makes it more likely that they invent new machines. Young emphasizes that what matters is that the simplification of certain phases of the production process will lead to the introduction of machines: "It is generally agreed that Adam Smith, when he suggested that the division of labor leads to inventions because workmen engaged in specialized routine operations come to see better ways of accomplishing the same results, missed the main point. The important thing, of course, is that with the division of labor a group of complex processes is transformed into a succession of simpler processes, some of which, at least, lend themselves to the use of machinery" (Young, 1928: 530).

8. Named after Verdoorn (1949) who found a strong empirical relationship between productivity growth and output growth in the industrial sectors.
9. For further discussion, see Ros (2000, 2013b).
10. Indeed, equation (2) and identity $q_{IND} = e_{IND} + p_{IND}$, where e_{IND} is the industrial employment growth rate, implies that $e_{IND} = -p_0/v + [(1-v)/v]p_{IND}$. For the relationship between employment and productivity growth to be positive this requires that $v < 1$.
11. This is so-called Kaldor's third law. See, on the subject, Kaldor (1966, 1967), Cripps and Tarling (1973) and Thirlwall (1983). For recent literature reviews on the subject, see Libanio (2006) and Moncayo (2011).
12. In addition there were several cases in which sudden and temporal changes in the wage share distorts the trend of TFP and coincide with years when, in reality GDP instead of being in a peak is falling or stagnant. In these cases, we used the GDP series to define the peak year.

3 THE REAL EXCHANGE RATE, THE REAL WAGE, AND GROWTH: A FORMAL ANALYSIS OF THE "DEVELOPMENT CHANNEL"

*Revised version of a paper prepared for the Conference honoring Roberto Frenkel, Buenos Aires, October 11–12, 2012. I am grateful to Carlos Ibarra, Carlo Panico and Martín Rapetti for comments on a previous version. The usual caveat applies.

1. In this economy the goods market equilibrium condition can be expressed as savings per unit of capital ($s_p r$) equals the sum of investment and net exports per unit of capital ($(1 - m)\, g + x$) where r is the profit rate equal to $(PY - WL)/P_I K$, g is the rate of capital accumulation (I/K), and x is the exports-capital ratio. This goods market equilibrium condition does not establish, however, a relationship between the rate of profit and the rate of accumulation. The profit rate is unaffected by the rate of capital accumulation. The reason is that changes in the rate of accumulation, which affect domestic demand, are reflected in changes in the exports-capital ratio, through the mechanism already discussed above, leaving the rate of profit unaffected.
2. Note that the r line is a horizontal line due to the assumption of perfect competition in both the foreign and the domestic market. With imperfect competition in the domestic market the r line

would slope upward since an increase in the rate of accumulation, by increasing domestic sales, shifts the composition of firms' sales from exports to the more profitable domestic market.

3. In Joan Robinson's words this is the "desired rate of accumulation," "a rate of accumulation which is generating just the expectation of profit that is required to cause it to be maintained" (Robinson, 1962, p. 130 in Sen, 1970).
4. Note that in this model the profit rate increases as a result of an increase in the output-capital ratio (the average productivity of capital) and not as a result of a redistribution against wage earners (employment increases in the same proportion as real wages fall).
5. These are directly taken from the arguments of Allyn Young and depend on the process of division of labor. See, on the subject, Lavezzi (2001).
6. For a formalization of Robinson's views, see Bhaduri (2006), Dutt (2006), and Dutt and Ros (2007).
7. In the case of reversible technical changes, this requires that the initial fall in the capital–labor ratio does not offset the positive effects on productivity of the increasing employment rate.

4 The Dutch Disease, the Staple Thesis, and the Recent Natural Resource Boom in South America

* A previous version of this paper was presented in the Workshop on New Developmentalism and a Structuralist Development Macroeconomics, organized by the Centro Celso Furtado, August 15–16, 2011, EESP, Fundação Getúlio Vargas, São Paulo, Brazil. I am grateful for comments to the participants in the workshop.

1. This specification is practically identical to that in Arrow's original model of learning by doing (Arrow, 1962) and is closely related to Romer's (1986) specification of a different kind of external effects (associated to Research and Development investments).
2. The real exchange rate is defined as the price ratio between tradable and nontradable goods. An appreciation means a fall in this ratio.
3. This requires, strictly speaking, the existence of multiple equilibria. See, on the subject, Krugman (1987), Ros and Skott (1998), Ros (2000, 2013b), and Rapetti (2011).
4. Qualitatively similar results can be derived from a Dixit-Stiglitz-Ethier type specification (used by Rodriguez-Clare, 1996).

5. The properties of the model are also similar to those in Berthelemy and Varoudakis (1996) except for the assumption in their model of an AK technology. In Berthelemy and Varoudakis the equivalent of our *I*-sector is a banking system that intermediates savings. Because it operates under economies of scale, the size of this sector is critical to the productivity of the whole economy.
6. As shown in Skott and Ros (1997), the price elasticity is given by: $-\partial \ln I_i / \partial \ln p_i = 1/(1-s) - (a+s-1)/n(1-s)a$.
7. If the LL and SS schedules do not intersect, there is a unique equilibrium without an *M* sector, that is, industrialization is not viable due to the small size of the labor force.
8. See Erten and Ocampo (2012) for an analysis of the recent cycle of commodity prices, the role of China's growth in it, and a comparison with previous cycles. As noted by these authors, commodity prices started to recover surprisingly fast after the interruption of the boom brought about by the crisis of 2008–2009. As a result, the world economy is experiencing again high commodity prices, which in a sense can be seen as part of the 2004–2008 boom.
9. See Frenkel and Rapetti (2011) for the construction of the indicator of unit labor costs in dollars.
10. Inflation targeting regimes now prevail in major Latin American countries. All six countries in Table 4.1 except Argentina have such regimes in place. Chile and Colombia were the pioneers having adopted inflation targets since 1990 and 1991 respectively. Peru introduced a floating exchange rate regime in 1994 and in 2002 the central bank replaced quantitative targets for monetary aggregates with inflation targets using the interest rate as the main instrument of monetary policy. After the 1994–1995 crisis, Mexico let the peso float and in 1999 moved to an inflation-targeting regime eventually adopting a target interest rate as policy instrument. Brazil also joined this group of countries in 1999 after the exchange rate crisis of the beginning of that year.
11. The so-called fear of floating may also contribute to this nonsymmetrical response and to a pro-cyclical management of interest rates. For a critical discussion of the suitability of inflation targeting for developing countries, see Epstein and Yeldan (2009) and Rapetti (2011). On the nonsymmetrical response of monetary policy to exchange rate shocks in the Mexican case, see Galindo and Ros (2008).

5 Close to the Epicenter: Mexico and Canada during the Great Recession

* I am grateful to Juan Carlos Moreno-Brid for comments to a previous version of this chapter. I also thank the excellent research assistance of Joaquín Cervantes, Elizabeth González and Luis Ángel Monroy Gómez Franco and the support of Martha Cordero from ECLAC-Mexico in the provision of indicators and statistical information on the trade performance of Canada and Mexico.

1. See, for example, Brown et al. (1991), Sobarzo (1991), and Young and Romero (1992). For a review and discussion of the studies of that time on this topic, see Lustig et al. (1992) and Ros (1992a, 1992b).
2. For further analysis of Mexico's economic development during the NAFTA period, see Moreno-Brid and Ros (2009).
3. The increase in unemployment is significant if one takes into account that the unemployment rate is usually very low in Mexico due to the definition of unemployment and the role of underemployment and the informal sector as adjustment mechanisms in the labor market in the face of employment reductions (see Frenkel and Ros, 2004, for further discussion).
4. On the decline of the bank credit to GDP ratio since the crisis of 1994–1995 in Mexico, see Moreno-Brid and Ros (2009).
5. For a detailed analysis of the fiscal measures in Canada, see OECD (2011), Cuevas (2011), and Canada's Economic Action Plan (2009). For a wider discussion of the fiscal measures of the Mexican government, see Ros (2011).
6. In the nontraditional measure of the national debt—that includes the net debt of the federal government, nonfinancial public companies, development banks, official trusts, and liabilities related to the restructuring of the banking system and PIDIREGAS—the debt coefficient to GDP was 40% at the end of 2008 (OECD, 2009b), also quite low for OECD standards.
7. It is also worth noting the role of development banks in relaxing credit restrictions that resulted from the financial crisis by providing financing to the most affected sectors (Banco de Mexico, 2010).
8. As a consequence of this depreciation, the real exchange rate at the beginning of 2009 was similar to the level of January 1997 when the economy was in full recovery and at the beginning of a period of four years in which GDP grew at a rate of more than 5% per year.
9. http://www.economist.com/blogs/dailychart/2011/08/gdp-recovery-recession

6 Why Does the Mexican Economy Grow Less Than That of Chile?

*Revised version of a paper presented in the "Sixth Dialogue for a Social Mexico," on November 19, 2013. I am grateful for comments to Rolando Cordera, Juan Carlos Moreno-Brid, and other conference participants. I am grateful also to Luis Angel Monroy Gómez Franco for excellent research assistance.

1. The trend is estimated with a Hodrick-Prescott (HP) filter.
2. The contrast is much greater if we compare the increase in the number of unemployed professionals (a rate of 15% per annum between 2000 and 2009) with the increase in the total number of unemployed (which grew at a rate of 10.1% per annum).
3. The six careers without serious problems of insufficient demand are nursing, geography, graphic design, biology and biotechnology, dentistry, and nutrition.
4. This is based on an estimated 7.1 million persons over the age of 14 with higher studies completed living in Mexico in 2007 (Hernández Laos et al., 2013).
5. The indicator was obtained as follows. The Penn World Table (PWT) 8.0 presents, for each year and country, the relationship between the exchange rate used for the conversion to purchasing power parity (PPP) and the market exchange rate (in national currency units per dollar). This is the variable pl_gdpo in the PWT that is inversely related to the real exchange rate: when the market exchange rate is relatively high with respect to the PPP exchange rate, the national currency is relatively depreciated and vice versa. To make comparable the real exchange rate among countries the method adopted by Rodrik (2008) was followed. This consists of adjusting for the Balassa-Samuelson effect in the following manner. First, a regression is run (for 11 Latin American countries with available information and years after circa 1990) between the inverse of pl_gdpo and GDP per capita: log (1/ pI_gdpo) = $a + b$log (GDP per capita). The result of the estimate shows a very significant Balassa-Samuelson effect: as GDP per capita increases the real exchange rate tends to fall (as the relative price of nontradables increases): log (1/ pI_gdpo) = 3.68 – 0.35 log (GDP per capita) R2 (aj.) = 0.27 N = 217, with a t-statistic equal to 9 in the GDP per capita coefficient, which implies that when per capita GDP increases by 10%, the real exchange rate appreciates by 3.5% (Rodrik obtains 2.4% in a much larger sample of countries). Second, with the predicted values for this regression for each country and year (log pred (1/ pI_gdpo))

the degree of undervaluation is obtained as log (1/ pI_gdpo) – log pred (1/ pI_gdpo) for each country and year. The average value of this variable is the one reported in the table.

6. Other factors that contributed to the decline in the growth rate were lower growth of the US economy and lower net financial flows, while a higher real price of oil had a positive effect on the growth rate.
7. For a critical discussion of the desirability of inflation targeting in developing countries, see Epstein and Yeldan (2009) and Rapetti (2011).
8. The reasons for the "fear to depreciate" are similar to those of the "fear of floating" (Calvo and Reinhart, 2002): the impact of depreciations on inflation and the increase in the real value of debt denominated in foreign currency, with the resulting financial difficulties for debtors and creditors.
9. The structural balance refers to the fiscal surplus adjusted for the effects of the economic cycle on public incomes and spending. Thus, if the structural balance is nil at all times during the business cycle, which implies a neutral fiscal policy, this means that the observed fiscal surplus must be negative in recessions and positive during booms.
10. Other studies that have documented the procyclical nature of fiscal policy in Mexico are Talvi and Végh (2000), World Bank (2001), and Kaminsky et al. (2004).

7 Mexico—Looking Ahead: Macroeconomic Policy and Development Strategy

1. Based on estimates of the nonresidential net capital stock provided by André Hofman.
2. Other factors contributing to the fall in the growth rate (of about 2.1 percentage points between the two periods) were a slower growth of the US economy and lower net financial inflows while a higher real oil price had a positive effect on the growth rate.
3. The mandate could of course also be changed in order to consider economic growth as an additional objective.
4. When the increase in foreign currency is associated with massive inflows of family remittances or sharp improvements in the terms of trade, the challenge of avoiding a persistent real exchange rate appreciation may be more complex but still manageable with appropriate interest rate management and intervention in the foreign exchange market.

References

Acemoglu, D., S. Johnson, Y. Thaicharoen, and J. Robinson (2003), Institutional causes, macroeconomic symptoms: Volatility, crisis and growth, *Journal of Monetary Economics*. 50(January 1): 49–123.

Acemoglu, D. and J. Robinson (2012), *Why Nations Fail?*, New York: Crown Publishers.

Aghion, P., R. Barro, and I. Marinescu (2006), *Cyclical Budgetary Policies: Their Determinants and Effects on Growth*. Mimeo Harvard University.

Aghion, P. and I. Marinescu (2006), *Cyclical Budgetary Policy and Economic Growth: What Do We Learn from OECD Panel Data?* Mimeo Harvard University.

Aghion, P. and P. Howitt (2009), *The Economics of Growth*. Cambridge, MA: MIT Press.

Arrow, K. J. (1962), The economic implications of learning by doing, *Review of Economic Studies* 29: 155–173.

Balassa, B. (1971), Trade policies in developing countries, *American Economic Review* 61(2): 178–187.

Banco de Mexico (2008), *Informe sobre la inflación*, Julio–Septiembre 2008, www.banxico.org.mx

Banco de Mexico (2010), *Informe anual 2009*, www.banxico.org.mx

Barbosa-Filho, Nelson (2008), Inflation targeting in Brazil: 1999–2006, *International Review of Applied Economics* 22: 187–200.

Barro, R. J. and J. W. Lee (2012), A new data set of educational attainment in the world, 1950–2010, *Journal of Development Economics* 104: 184–198.

Basu, K. (1997), Analytical Development Economics. The Less Developed Economy Revisited, Cambridge: The MIT Press.

Basu, S. and D. Weil (1998), Appropriate technology and growth, *Quarterly Journal of Economics* 113(4): 1025–1054.

Benhabib, J. and M. M. Spiegel (1994), The role of human capital in economic development: Evidence from aggregate cross-country data, *Journal of Monetary Economics* 34: 143–173.

Benhabib, J. and M. M. Spiegel (2005), Technological diffusion and economic growth. In P. Aghion and S. Durlauf (eds.), *Handbook of Economic Growth*. Amsterdam: Elsevier.

Berthelemy, J. C. and A. Varoudakis (1996), Economic growth, convergence clubs, and the role of financial development, *Oxford Economic Papers* 48: 300–328.

Bhaduri, A. (2006), Endogenous economic growth: a new approach, *Cambridge Journal of Economics* 30: 69–83

Bhaduri, A. and S. Marglin (1990), Unemployment and the real wage: The economic basis for contesting political ideologies, *Cambridge Journal of Economics* 14: 375–393.

Bhagwati, J. N. (1985), *Essays on Development Economics*, Vol. 1. Cambridge, MA: The MIT Press.

Blanchflower, D. and A. Oswald (1994), *The Wage Curve*. Cambridge, MA: MIT Press.

Blanchflower, D. and A. Oswald (2005), The Wage Curve Reloaded, NBER Working Paper.

Blecker, R. (2009), External shocks, structural change, and economic growth in Mexico, 1979–2007, *World Development* 37(7): 1274–1284.

Bordo, M., A. Redish, and H. Rockoff (2011), Why didn't Canada have a banking crisis in 2008 (or in 1930, or 1907, or…)? NBER Working Paper No. 17312.

Bresser-Pereira, L. C. (2008), Dutch disease and its neutralization: A Ricardian approach, *Brazilian Journal of Political Economy* 28(1): 47–71.

Bresser-Pereira, L. C. (2011), From old to new developmentalism. In J. A. Ocampo and J. Ros (eds.), *Oxford Handbook of Latin American Economics*. Oxford: Oxford University Press.

Brown, D., A. Deardorff, and R. Stern (1991), A North American Free Trade Agreement: Analytical Issues and a Computational Assessment. Manuscrito no publicado.

Bulmer-Thomas, V. (2003), *The Economic History of Latin America since Independence*, Cambridge: Cambridge University Press.

Burgstaller, A. and N. Saavedra-Rivano (1984), Capital mobility and growth in a North–South model, *Journal of Development Economics* 15: 213–237.

Calderón, C. and L. Servén (2004), Trends in Infrastructure in Latin America, 1980–2001, The World Bank, Policy Research Working Paper Series: 3401.

Calderón, C. and L. Servén (2011), Infrastructure in Latin America. In J. A. Ocampo and J. Ros (eds.), *The Oxford Handbook of Latin American Economics*. Oxford: Oxford University Press.

Calvo, G. and C. Reinhart (2002), Fear of floating, *Quarterly Journal of Economics* 117(2): 379–408.

Canada's Economic Action Plan (2009), (available in http://www.actionplan.gc.ca/eng/feature.asp?pageId=90)

Carreras de Velasco, M. (1974), *Los mexicanos que devolvió la crisis, 1929–1932*, México: Secretaría de Relaciones Exteriores.

Carton, C. (2009), Kaldorian mechanisms of regional growth: An empirical application to the case of ALADOI 1980–2007, MPRA paper No. 15675.

Casar, J. and J. Ros (2004), ¿Porqué no crecemos?, *Nexos*, Octubre.

Cavallo, D. F., J. A. Cottani, and M. S. Kahn (1990), Real exchange rate behavior and economic performance in LDCs, *Economic Development and Cultural Change* 39(October): 61–76.

CEPAL (2000), *Equidad, Desarrollo y Ciudadanía*. Santiago de Chile: CEPAL.

CEPAL (2001), *Panorama Social de América Latina, 2000–2001*. Santiago de Chile: CEPAL.

CEPAL (2009), *Balance preliminar de las economias de América Latina y el Caribe*. Santiago de Chile: CEPAL.

CEPAL (2014), *Pactos para la Igualdad*, Santiago de Chile: Naciones Unidas.

Chiquiar, D. and M. Ramos Francia (2009), *Competitividad y crecimiento en la economía mexicana*. Banco de México, Documentos de Investigación No. 2009–11.

Corden, W. M. (1984), Booming sector and Dutch disease economics: Survey and consolidation, *Oxford Economic Papers* 36: 359–380.

Corden, W. M. and J. P. Neary (1982), Booming sector and deindustrialization in a small open economy, *Economic Journal* 92: 825–848.

Cripps, T. F., and R. J. Tarling (1973), *Growth in Advanced Capitalist Economies 1950–1970*. Cambridge: Cambridge University Press.

Cuevas, V. M. (2011), Mexico y Canada ante la crisis financiera estadounidense: un estudio comparativo, *Economía UNAM* 8(24): 51–77.

Darity, W. and L. Davis (2005), Growth, trade and uneven development, *Cambridge Journal of Economics* 29: 141–170.

Dávila, E., G. Kessel, and S. Levy (2002), El sur también existe: un ensayo sobre el desarrollo regional de México, *Economía Mexicana Nueva Época* XI(2), segundo semestre: 205–260.

Denison, E. (1967), *Why Growth Rates Differ. Postwar Experience in Nine Western Countries*. Washington, DC: Brookings Institution.

Díaz-Alejandro, C. (1965), *Exchange Rate Devaluation in a Semi-Industrialized Country*. Cambridge, VT: MIT Press.

Díaz-Alejandro, C. (1988), No less than one hundred years of Argentine economic history plus some comparisons, in A. Velasco (ed.), *Trade, Development and the World Economy. Selected Essays of Carlos F. Díaz-Alejandro*, Oxford and NY: B. Blackwell.

Dollar, D. (1986), Technological innovation, capital mobility, and the product cycle in North–South trade, *American Economic Review* (March): 177–190.

Dollar, D. (1992), Outward-oriented developing economies really do grow more rapidly: Evidence from 95 LDCs, 1976–1985, *Economic Development and Cultural Change* 40: 523–544.

Dutt, A. (1984), Stagnation, income distribution, and monopoly power, *Cambridge Journal of Economics* 8: 25–40.

Dutt, A. (1988), North–South models: A critical survey, unpublished, Department of Economics, University of Notre Dame.

Dutt, A. (1990), *Growth, Distribution and Uneven Development*. Cambridge: Cambridge University Press.

Dutt, A. (1996), Southern primary exports, technological change and uneven development, *Cambridge Journal of Economics* 20: 73–89.

Dutt, A. (2003), Income elasticities of imports: North–South trade and uneven development. In A. Dutt and J. Ros (eds.), *Development Economics and Structuralist Macroeconomics*. Cheltenham, UK and Northampton, MA: Edward Elgar.

Dutt, A. K. (2006), Aggregate demand, aggregate supply and economic growth, *International Review of Applied Economics*, 20(3), July, 319–336.

Dutt, A. K. and J. Ros (2007). Aggregate demand shocks and economic growth, *Structural Change and Economic Dynamics*, 18(1), March, 75–99.

Easterly, W. and R. Levine (2001), What have we learned from a decade of empirical research on growth? It's not factor accumulation: Stylized facts and growth models, *World Bank Economic Review* 15(2): 177–219.

ECLAC (2005), *CAN: análisis de la competitividad de los países, programa computacional para evaluar y describir el medio competitivo internacional*. Santiago de Chile: ECLAC.

Eichengreen, B. (2007), The Real Exchange Rate and Economic Growth, Commission on Growth and Development, Working Paper No 4.

Epstein, G. and E. Yeldan (2009), *Beyond Inflation Targeting: Assessing the Impacts and Policy Alternatives*. Cheltenham, UK: Edward Elgar Publishing.

Erten, B. and J. A. Ocampo (2012), Super-cycles of commodity prices since the mid nineteenth century, DESA Working Paper 110, February.

Esquivel, G. (2010), De la inestabilidad macroeconómica al estancamiento estabilizador: El papel del diseño y conducción de la política económica en México, N. Lustig (coord.), *Crecimiento Económico y Equidad, vol. IX de Los Grandes Problemas de México*, El Colegio de México.

Faal, E. (2005), GDP growth, potential output, and output gaps in Mexico, IMF Working Paper, WP/05/93.

Fanelli, J. M., R. Frenkel, and G. Rozenwurcel (1993), Crecimiento y reforma estructural en América Latina. La situación actual, en J. Ros (coord.), *La Edad de Plomo del Desarrollo Latinoamericano*. México, D. F.: FCE.

Feenstra, R. C., R. Inklaar, and M. P. Timmer (2013), The Next Generation of the Penn World Table, disponible en www.ggdc.net/pwt

Findlay, R. (1980), The terms of trade and equilibrium growth in the world economy, *American Economic Review* (June): 291–299.

Frenkel, R. (2004), *Real Exchange rate and employment in Argentina, Brazil, Chile and Mexico*. Buenos Aires: CEDES. Paper prepared for the G24.

Frenkel, R. (2008), The competitive real exchange-rate regime, inflation and monetary policy, *Cepal Review* 96: 191–201.

Frenkel, R. and J. Ros (2004), Desempleo, políticas macroeconómicas y flexibilidad del mercado laboral. Argentina y México en los noventa, *Desarrollo Económico* 44(173) (April–June): 36–53.

Frenkel, R. and J. Ros (2006), Unemployment and the real exchange rate in Latin America, *World Development* 34(4): 631–646.

Frenkel, R. and M. Rapetti (2004), *Políticas macroeconómicas para el crecimiento y el empleo*, paper prepared for the ILO.

Frenkel, R. and M. Rapetti (2011), La principal amenaza de América Latina en la próxima década: ¿fragilidad externa o primarización?, Serie Macroeconomía del Desarrollo 116, Noviembre. Santiago, Chile: CEPAL.

Frenkel, R. and M. Rapetti (2012), External fragility or deindustrialization: What is the main threat to Latin American countries in the 2010s? *World Economic Review* 1: 37–57.

Gala, P. (2008), Real exchange rate levels and economic development: Theoretical analysis and econometric evidence, *Cambridge Journal of Economics* 32(2): 273.

Galindo, L. M. and J. Ros (2008), Alternatives to inflation targeting in Mexico, *International Review of Applied Economics* 22(2): 201–214.

Giugale, Marcelo, Olivier Lafourcade, and Vinh H. Nguyen (eds.) (2001), *Mexico. A Comprehensive Development Agenda for the New Era*. Washington, DC: The World Bank.

Hausmann, R., J. Hwang, and D. Rodrik (2005), What you export matters, NBER Working Paper 11905.

Hernández Laos, E., R. Solís, and A. Stefanovich (2013), *Mercado Laboral de Profesionistas en México*. México: ANUIES.

Ibarra, C. 2010, Capital flows, real exchange rate, and growth constraints in Mexico, Department of Economics, Universidad de las Américas, Mimeo.

IMF (2009), The State of Public Finances Cross-Country Fiscal Monitor, November 2009, IMF Staff Position Note, Prepared by the Staff of the Fiscal Affairs Department. Washington, DC: IMF.

IMF (2010a), World Economic Outlook Update, January 2010.

IMF (2010b), Staff report for the 2010 Article IV Consultation, March 1, 2010.

IMF (2010c), Mexico. Arrangement under the flexible credit line and cancellation of the current arrangement, March 17, 2010.

Izquierdo, A. and E. Talvi (coord.) (2011), *One Region, Two Speeds?* Washington, DC: IDB.

Jácome, L. and F. Vázquez (2005), Any Link Between Legal Central Bank Independence and Inflation? Evidence from Latin America and the Caribbean, IMF Working Paper WP/05/75. Washington, DC: IMF.

Jorgenson, D. and Z. Griliches (1967), The explanation of productivity change, *Review of Economic Studies* XXXIV: 249–283.

Kaldor, N. (1957), A model of economic growth, *Economic Journal* 67: 591–624.

Kaldor, N. (1966), *Causes of the Slow Rate of Economic Growth of the United Kingdom*. Cambridge: Cambridge University Press.

Kaldor, N. (1967), *Strategic Factors in Economic Development*, The Frank W. Pierce Memorial Lectures at Cornell University, October 1966, Cornell University, Ithaca, NY.

Kaldor, N. (1968), Productivity and growth in manufacturing industry: A reply, *Economica* 35: 385–391.

Kaldor, N. (1971), Conflicts in national economic objectives, *Economic Journal* 81 (March): 321.

Kaldor, N. (1972), The irrelevance of equilibrium economics, *Economic Journal* 82(328): 1237–1255.

Kaldor, N. (1975), What is wrong with economic theory?, *Quarterly Journal of Economics* 89(3): 347–357.

Kaldor, N. (1976), Inflation and recession in the world economy, *Economic Journal* 86: 703–714.

Kaldor, N. (1979), Equilibrium theory and growth theory. In M. Baskin (ed.), *Economics and Human Welfare—Essays in Honour of Tibor Scitovsky*. New York: Academic Press.

Kaldor, N. (1981), The role of increasing returns, technical progress and cumulative causation, Economie Appliquée, 4. Reprinted in Kaldor, N. (1989), *Further Essays on Economic Theory and Policy*, pp. 201–223. London: Ducksworth.

Kaldor, N. (1985), *Economics without Equilibrium*. Cardiff, UK: University College Cardiff Press.

Kaminsky, G., C. Reinhart, and C. Végh (2004), When it rains, it pours: Procyclical capital flows and macroeconomic policies, NBER Working Paper No. 10780.

Klenow, P. and A. Rodriguez-Clare (1997), The neoclassical revival in growth economics: Has it gone too far. In B. Bernanke and J. Rotenberg (eds.), *NBER Macroeconomics Annual 1997*. Cambridge, MA: MIT Press.

Krueger, A. and M. Lindahl (2001), Education for growth: Why and for whom?, *Journal of Economic Literature* 39(4): 1101–1136.

Krugman, P. (1979), A model of innovation, technology transfer, and the world distribution of income, *Journal of Political Economy* 87(2): 253–266.

Krugman, P. (1987), The narrow moving band, the Dutch disease, and the competitive consequences of Mrs. Thatcher, *Journal of Development Economics* 27(1–2): 41–55.

Lachler, U. and D. Aschauer (1998), Public investment and economic growth in Mexico, Policy Research Working Paper 1964, World Bank.

Lavezzi, A. (2001), Division of labor and economic growth: from Adam Smith to Paul Romer and beyond, University of Pisa, unpublished

Levy-Yeyati, E. and F. Sturzenegger (2009), Fear of appreciation: Exchange rate policy as a development strategy. In G. Hammond, R. Kanbur, and E. Prasad (eds.), *Monetary Policy Frameworks for Emerging Markets*. Cheltenham, UK: Edward Elgar Publishing.

Lewis, W. A. (1954), Economic development with unlimited supplies of labour, *The Manchester School* 28: 139–191.

Libanio, G. (2006), Three Essays on Aggregate Demand and Growth, Ph.D. Dissertation, University of Notre Dame.

Loayza, N., Fajnzylber, P., and C. Calderón (2005), *Economic Growth in Latin America and the Caribbean*. Washington, DC: The World Bank.

Lora, E. (2001), Structural Reforms in Latin America: What Has Been Reformed and How to Measure it, IADB Research Department Working Paper No. 466. Washington, DC: IADB.

Lora, Eduardo and Carmen Pagés (1996), *Legislación laboral en el proceso de reformas estructurales de América Latina y el Caribe*. Washington, DC: BID.

Lucas, R. E., Jr. (1988), On the mechanics of economic development, *Journal of Monetary Economics* 22: 3–42.

Lustig, N. (2000), Crises and the poor: Socially responsible macroeconomics, *Economia* 1(1): 1–19.

Lustig, N., B. P. Bosworth, and R. Z. Lawrence (eds.) (1992), *North American Free Trade*. Washington, DC: Brookings Institution.

Maddison, A. (2007), *Historical Statistics for the World Economy: 1-2003 AD*, GGDC databases (http:www.ggdc.net/), update of A. Maddison (2003), *The World Economy: Historical Statistics*, Paris, OECD Development Centre Studies.

Maddison, A. (2009), *Historical Statistics for the World Economy*, GGDC databases (http:www.ggdc.net/), update of A. Maddison (2003), *The World Economy: Historical Statistics*, Paris, OECD Development Centre Studies.

Mankiw, G., D. Romer, and D. Weil (1992), A contribution to the empirics of economic growth, *Quarterly Journal of Economics* 107: 407–437.

Molana, H. and D. Vines (1989), North–South growth and the terms of trade: A model on Kaldorian lines, *Economic Journal* 99(June): 443–453.

Moncayo, E. (2011), Cambio estructural, crecimineto e industrialización en América Latina, 1950–2005, Tesis de doctorado, Universidad Nacional de Colombia.

Moreno-Brid, J. C. and J. Ros (2009), *Development and Growth in the Mexican Economy. A Historical Perspective*. Oxford: Oxford University Press.

Moreno-Brid, J. C., J. Santamaría, and J. C. Rivas (2005), Industrialization and economic growth in Mexico after NAFTA: The road traveled, *Development and Change* 36(6): 1095–1119.

Morgan Stanley (2010), Economics. This week in Latin America, January 19, 2010.

Murillo, M., L. Ronconi, and A. Schrank (2011), Latin American labor reforms: Evaluating risk and security. In J. A. Ocampo and

J. Ros (eds.), *The Oxford Handbook of Latin American Economics.* Oxford: Oxford University Press.

Nelson, R. and E. Phelps (1966), Investment in humans, technological diffusion and economic growth, *American Economic Review* 56: 69–75.

Ocampo, J. A. (2003), Developing countries' anti-cyclical policies in a globalized world. In A. Dutt and J. Ros (eds.), *Development Economics and Structuralist Macroeconomics. Essays in Honor of Lance Taylor.* Cheltenham, UK: Edward Elgar.

Ocampo, J. A. (2004), Latin America's growth and equity frustrations during structural reforms, *Journal of Economic Perspectives* 18(2), (Spring): 67–88.

Ocampo, J. A. and J. Malagón (2011), El tamaño del estado y su impacto redistributivo en América Latina, CAF Documentos de Trabajo No 2011/11.

Ocampo, J. A. and J. Ros (2011), Shifting paradigms in Latin America's economic development. In J. A. Ocampo and J. Ros (eds.), *The Oxford Handbook of Latin American Economics.* Oxford: Oxford University Press.

OECD (2007), *Getting It Right: OECD Perspectives on Policy Challenges in Mexico.* Paris: OECD.

OECD (2009a), *Economic Survey of Mexico 2009*, OECD.

OECD (2009b), *OECD Review of Budgeting in Mexico*, volume 2009/Supplement 1, OECD.

OECD (2009c), Economic Outlook. Interim Report, March 2009. OECD.

OECD (2011), *Economic Survey. Canada. 2010.* OECD.

Pacheco-López, P. and A. P. Thirlwall (2013), A new interpretation of Kaldor's first growth law for open developing economies, School of Economics Discussion Paper, University of Kent.

Pagés, C. (ed.) (2010), *La Era de la Productividad.* Washington, DC: BID.

Pastor, J. and A. Villagómez (2007), The structural budget balance: A preliminary estimation for Mexico, *Applied Economics* 39(12): 1599–1607.

Perrotti, D. and R. Sánchez (2011), *La brecha de infraestructura en América Latina y el Caribe*, Serie Recursos Naturales e Infraestructura. Santiago de Chile: CEPAL.

Pew Hispanic Center (2009), *Mexican Immigrants: How Many Come? How Many Leave?* Washington, DC: Pew Research Center.

Polterovich, V. and V. Popov (2002), Accumulation of foreign exchange reserves and long term growth, *New Economic School*, Moscow, Russia.

Porcile, G. and G. T. Lima (2010), Real Exchange Rate and Elasticity of Labour Supply in a Balance-of-Payments-Constrained Macrodynamics. *Cambridge Journal of Economics*, 34, 1019–1039.

Prasad, E., R. Rajan, and A. Subramanian (2007), Foreign capital and economic growth, *Brookings Papers on Economic Activity*, 1: 153–209.

Prebisch, R. (1950), *The Economic Development of Latin America and Its Principal Problems.* Lake Success, NY: United Nations.

Pritchett, L. (2001), Where has all the education gone? *World Bank Economic Review* 15(3): 367–393.

Przeworski, Adam (2004), Democracy and economic development. In E. D. Mansfield and Richard Sisson (eds.), *The Evolution of Political Knowledge*. Columbus: Ohio State University Press.

Rada, C. and L. Taylor (2006), Empty sources of growth accounting, and empirical replacements a la Kaldor and Goodwin with some beef, *Structural Change and Economic Dynamics* 17: 486–500.

Ramirez, M. (2004), Is public infrastructure investment productive in the Mexican case? A vector error correction analysis, *Journal of International Trade and Economic Development* 13(2): 159–178.

Rapetti, M. (2011), *Macroeconomic Policy Coordination in a Competitive Real Exchange Rate Strategy for Development.* Working Paper 2011–09. Amherst, MA: University of Massachusetts.

Rapetti, M. (2012), *Real Exchange Rate Levels and Economic Growth: Some Reflections on the Possible Channels.* Buenos Aires: CEDES. Mimeo.

Rapetti, M., P. Skott, and A. Razmi (2012), The real exchange rate and economic growth: Are developing countries different? *International Review of Applied Economics* 26(6): 735–753.

Razin, O. and S. Collins (1997), *Real Exchange Rate Misalignments and Growth*, NBER Working Paper 6147. National Bureau of Economic Research.

Razmi, A., M. Rapetti, and P. Skott (2012), The real exchange rate and economic development, *Structural Change and Economic Dynamics* 23(2): 151–169.

Robinson, J. (1956) *Accumulation of capital*, London: Macmillan.

Robinson, J. (1962), A model of accumulation, in *Essays in the Theory of Economic Growth*, Macmillan, pp. 34–59.

Rodriguez-Clare, A. (1996), The division of labor and economic development, *Journal of Development Economics* 49: 3–32.

Rodrik, D. (2008), The real exchange rate and economic growth, *Brookings Papers on Economic Activity* 2: 365–412.

Romer, P. M. (1986), Increasing returns and long-run growth, *Journal of Political Economy* 94: 1002–1037.

Romer, P. M. (1990), Endogenous technological change, *Journal of Political Economy* 98 (part 2): 71–102.

Ros, J. (1992a), NAFTA: Free trade area or common capital market? *Journal of Interamerican Studies and World Affairs* 2 (Summer): 53–91.

Ros, J. (1992b), Comment on Weintraub, "NAFTA and Industry." In N. Lustig, B. P. Bosworth, and R. Z. Lawrence (eds.), *North American Free Trade*. Washington, DC: Brookings Institution.

Ros, J. (1994), Beneficios comerciales y movilidad de capital: Estudios recientes sobre las consecuencias del TLC, *Comercio Exterior* 44(6), (Junio): 498–501.

Ros, J. (2000), *Development Theory and the Economics of Growth*. Ann Arbor: University of Michigan Press.

Ros, J. (2006), Changing growth constraints in Northern Latin America. In A. Solimano (ed.), *Vanishing Growth in Latin America: The Late Twentieth Century Experience*. Cheltenham, UK: Edward Elgar.

Ros, J. (2008), La desaceleración del crecimiento económico en México desde 1982, *El Trimestre Económico* 75(299): 1–32.

Ros, J. (2009), Reducción de la pobreza en América Latina: el papel del crecimiento, la distribución del ingreso, el gasto social y el cambio demográfico, *Revista de la CEPAL* 98(Agosto): 35–45.

Ros, J. (2011), The economic crisis of 2008–2009 and development strategy: The Mexican case. In M. Haddad and B. Shepherd (eds.), *Managing Openness. Trade and Outward-Oriented Growth After the Crisis*. Washington, DC: The World Bank.

Ros, J. (2013a), *Algunas Tesis Equivocadas sobre el Estancamiento Económico de México*. México: El Colegio de México-UNAM.

Ros, J. (2013b), *Rethinking Economic Development, Growth, and Institutions*. Oxford: Oxford University Press.

Ros, J. and P. Skott (1998), Dynamic effects of trade liberalization and currency overvaluation under conditions of increasing returns, *The Manchester School* 66(4): 466–489.

Saavedra-Rivano, N. (1982), North–South models and capital mobility, unpublished Ph. D. dissertation, Columbia University.

Sachs, J. and A. Warner (2001), The curse of natural resources, *European Economic Review* 45: 827–838.

Secretaría de Hacienda y Crédito Público (SHCP) (2010a), *Criterios Generales de Política Económica 2010*. Mexico: SHCP.

Secretaría de Hacienda y Crédito Público (SHCP) (2010b), *Informe Semanal. Del 22 al 26 de marzo de 2010*. Mexico: SHCP.

Secretaría de Hacienda y Crédito Público (SHCP) (2011), *Criterios Generales de Política Económica 2011*. Mexico: SHCP.

Sen, A. (1970) (ed), *Growth Economics*, Penguin Books

Singer, H. (1950), The distribution of gains between investing and borrowing countries, *American Economic Review* 40(2): May.

Sistema Económico Latinoamericano (SELA) (2009), *La emigración de recursos humanos calificados desde países de América Latina y el Caribe. Tendencias contemporáneas y perspectivas*. Junio.

Skott, P. and J. Ros (1997), The 'big push' in an open economy with non tradable inputs, *Journal of Post Keynesian Economics* 20: 149–62

Smith, A. (1776), *An Inquiry into the Nature and Causes of the Wealth of Nations*, E. Cannan edition. New York: G. P. Putnam's Sons, 1904.

Sobarzo, H. (1991), *Análisis de los efectos de un Tratado de Libre Comercio entre Mexico y América del Norte: Un enfoque de Equilibrio General*. Mexico: El Colegio de Mexico, Centro de Estudios Económicos.

Solow, R. M. (1956), A contribution to the theory of economic growth, *Quarterly Journal of Economics* 70: 65–94.

Solow, R. M. (1957), Technical change and the aggregate production function, *Review of Economics and Statistics* 79(3): 367–370.

Sosa, S. (2008), External shocks and business cycle fluctuations in Mexico: How important are US factors? IMF Working Paper No. 08/100. International Monetary Fund.

Stallings, B. and J. Weller (2001), Employment in Latin America: Cornerstone of social policy, *CEPAL Review*, no. 75, LC/G.2150-P, Santiago, Chile, December.

Suescún, R. (2007), *The Size and Effectiveness of the Automatic Fiscal Stabilizers in Latin America, and Fiscal Policy, Stabilization, and Growth: Prudence or Abstinence?* Washington, DC: The World Bank.

Swan, T. W. (1956), Economic growth and capital accumulation, *Economic Record* LXVI: 334–361.

Talvi, E. and C. Végh (2000), *Tax Base Variability and Procyclical Fiscal Policy*, NBER Working Paper No. 7499.

Taylor, L. (1981), South–North trade and Southern growth: Bleak prospects from a structuralist point of view, *Journal of International Economics* 11: 589–602.

Taylor, L. (1983), *Structuralist Macroeconomics*. New York: Basic Books.

Thirlwall, A. P. (1983), A plain man's guide to Kaldor's laws, *Journal of Post Keynesian Economics* 5: 345–358.

Timmer, M. P. and G. J. de Vries (2007), Groningen Growth and Development Center 10 sector database, June 2007, http://www.ggdc.net/

United Nations (2006), *World Economic and Social Survey 2006: Diverging Growth and Development.* New York: United Nations.

Vega, M. (2005), *La Reforma Laboral en América Latina: 15 años después. Un análisis comparado*, Lima: OIT, Oficina Regional para América Latina y el Caribe.

Verdoorn, P. J. (1949), Fattori che regolano lo sviluppo della produttivita del lavoro (Factors governing the growth of labor productivity), *L'Industria* 1: 3–10 (English translation by A. P. Thirlwall and G. Thirlwall (1979) in *Research in Population and Economics*).

Villagómez, A. and J. Orellana (2009), *Monetary Policy Rules in a Small Open Economy: An Application to Mexico*, Working Paper, Tecnológico de Monterrey.

Vines, D. (1984), "A North-South Growth Model along Kaldorian Lines", Discussion Paper Series, No. 26, Centre for Economic Policy Research.

World Bank (1995), *Bureaucrats in Business*, World Bank Policy Research Report #4. Washington, DC: World Bank.

World Bank (2001), *Fiscal policy, business cycles and growth in Mexico: Fiscal sustainability*, Report No. 20236-ME. Washington, DC: World Bank.

World Bank (2009), *Doing Business*, Washington, DC: World Bank.

World Bank (2013), *Doing Business*, Washington, DC: World Bank.

Young, A. (1928), Increasing returns and economic progress, *Economic Journal* 38: 527–542.

Young, L. and J. Romero (1992), *Steady Growth and Transition in a Dynamic Dual Model of the North American Free Trade Agreement.* Unpublished manuscript.

Index

CPSIA information can be obtained
at www.ICGtesting.com
Printed in the USA
BVOW06*1433281117
501470BV00012B/423/P

9 781137 465269